WHEN GOD IS FIRST

MIKE HAYES

ALBURY PUBLISHING
Tulsa, OK

CRITICAL ACCLAIM

"Pastor Mike Hayes' teaching ministry has consistently been marked by revelatory insight into the powerful truths of Scripture. He has particularly excelled in his gift to communicate faith in the sensitive area of the kingdom of God and money.

"No serious Christian should be without this body of teaching."

Bishop Joseph L. Garlington
Senior Pastor
Covenant Church of Pittsburgh
Pittsburgh, Pennsylvania

"Mike Hayes' message on "first fruits" is compelling, convincing and convicting. I have studied the Bible for years, heard sermons all my life and have six academic degrees, yet I had never heard this amazing biblical concept until Mike preached the sermon. I found myself sitting on the edge of my seat thinking, 'How come I have never heard this before?' But that question was superceded by, 'How can I learn to apply this in my life?'

"I'm ecstatic this concept is finally in book form. This concept is one of those few that is truly life changing".

Dr. Jim Garlow
Senior Pastor
Skyline Wesleyan Church
San Diego, California

CRITICAL ACCLAIM

"In 19 years of pastoring Jubilee Christian Center, I can truthfully say Pastor Mike Hayes' message on first things was the most life changing sermon we ever heard.

"Every serious believer must read this book!"

**Dick Bernal
Senior Pastor
Jubilee Christian Center
San Jose, California**

"Pastor Mike Hayes' message, "The Devoted Thing," is one of the most revolutionary, relevant, relative and revelatory messages I've ever heard on the subject of tithing and first fruits. His deeply prophetic and insightful message strongly impacted our church causing our weekly giving to increase by more than 20 percent each week, which still continues.

"No pastor, no elder, no Christian should be without this powerful tool that is guaranteed to forever change your perspective on the message and practice of tithing and
first fruits giving."

**Bishop Carlton D. Pearson
Presiding Bishop, Azusa Fellowship International
Senior Pastor, Higher Dimensions Family Church
Tulsa, Oklahoma**

2nd Printing

When God Is First
Transform Your Life Through His Promises

ISBN 1-57778-217-8

Copyright © 2000
by MIKE HAYES
2644 East Trinity Mills Road
Carrollton, TX 75006

Published by ALBURY PUBLISHING
P.O. Box 470406
Tulsa, OK 74147-0406

Cover design, interior format and typesetting by:
Paragon Communications Group, Inc., Tulsa, Oklahoma

DEDICATION

*I would make no other dedication than to my wife
and dearest friend Kathy. She is the most loving,
faithful and balanced person I have ever known.
Next to the Holy Spirit,
God has given me no greater gift.
Thank you sweetheart for
all you are!*

ACKNOWLEDGEMENTS

I wish to thank from the bottom of my heart my daughter Amie, for her dedication to this project. She has taken it on as a personal challenge, feeling the same sense of urgency that I have about the importance of the message getting out.

Also, thank you to; Denise Glenn, George Spillman and his wife Karyn, Andria Ayers, Amy Hossler, Karen Geer and Stacey Dockery for their tireless commitment to the completion of this book. I could not have done it without them.

FOREWORD

Have you ever felt the hot sting of childhood rejection? Some of us will remember well the pain of being chosen last for schoolyard sports. Imagine the ache of standing there with your classmates, hope fading into despair as one-by-one everyone is chosen but you. "Pick me...Pick me" the youngster chants with hope their, their little heart...but the fear in their eyes pleads, "Don't let me be last...spare me the indignity of not being chosen."

Now imagine our Creator on the cross, hands outstretched as if to say, "choose me...put me first!" The Holy Writ is filled with admonitions to put "first the kingdom of God." But often we leave the most valuable player standing there, overlooked — trying everything and everyone else first. And then still have the audacity to wonder why we don't win at life!

What happens *"When God is First?"* Many Christians say He's first in their lives, but their walk doesn't match their talk. My friend Mike Hayes is a shining exception: his walk equals his talk. He has discovered the Biblical principle of first fruits. Not everybody that makes an amazing discovery has the ability to explain it to others. Mike has that ability.

This book is a roadmap to a land that flows with milk and honey...the promised land — the place where God's order is honored and His people are blessed. Everybody wants to live in the promised

WHEN GOD IS FIRST

land, but few are willing to travel the road that takes you there.

When God is First leads you step-by-step, principle-by-principle, to the land of God's fulfilled promises.

Read it...then try it!

See what happens when God is first!

Tommy Tenney
God Chasers Network

Contents

INTRODUCTION

This day was not unlike any other day for the pastor of a small fledgling church. Check the appointment book, make a few phone calls and spend a little time praying in preparation for whatever the day would hold. What I wasn't prepared for, however, was the events that this simple day would set in motion.

When Bill and Kathleen walked into my office I wasn't sure what the purpose of their visit was. I knew their marriage was suspect at times, but many young couples need counsel when a marriage is new. As I was soon to learn, this time their problem was not marriage.

"Pastor", they began, "we have a question. We do not understand why we faithfully pay our tithes to support our church and we are not being blessed. Most of the time we cannot pay all of our bills. If something doesn't change, we will be forced to file for bankruptcy. What are we doing wrong?"

I knew this family to be hard working, faithful people and their giving seemed to be especially consistent. I thought of every possible reason and checked it off in my mind. I didn't want to send them away without an answer. After all, I was a young pastor desiring to be the source of all inspired information. Even still, I felt that there was something to be learned on my part. So, I admitted that I did not have the solution for them. I did promise, however, to pray about it and try to help them with an answer.

After they left my office I slumped back into my chair and drifted off into thought. Reviewing the facts, I knew one thing was sure - God is faithful and His Word is true. So if the promised results of obedience to God's word were not happening, it wasn't God's fault.

If I hadn't known Bill and Kathleen so well, I probably would have spouted off the same old things I knew about giving. But this was different. They were practicing what I had been preaching to them. As I remember, about two weeks later I called the couple back into my office to ask them some specific questions.

I asked Bill to describe to me the process from the time they received their paycheck to the moment their tithe touched the offering plate. By the end of the conversation, our confusion was gone, replaced by the overwhelming clarity of the answer. The revelation realized in my little office not only changed the course of this couples' lives, but also affected the destiny of our church and thousands of lives forever. After all, our church at that time served about 200 members and we were struggling to keep what we had.

Now, a few years later, we have experienced more of God's blessing than we ever dreamed possible. We now have an annual budget of millions of dollars and a membership approaching 10,000, worshipping weekly on a campus of more than 40 prime acres. Our church has birthed a school filled with world class faculty and fields a sports program of championship caliber.

I am so humbled to see what God has done! I only played a small part by stepping out in faith 25 years ago, with my wife Kathy. I believe if I can be successful, anyone can. I also believe that the secret uncovered in this book has been one of the most important ingredients in our success.

As you begin reading, you may ask yourself, "Why didn't he just tell us what to do to be blessed? Couldn't I have gotten the point without being dragged through ancient Bible stories?"

Let me answer that with a question of my own. "If you not only had the instructions but understood the reasons behind them, would that understanding dramatically increase the importance you placed on obeying those instructions?"

In 1947, my father was a young U.S. Navy recruit. World War II had just ended and the ship he was stationed aboard stopped in the Philippines for an airshow celebration. Although my dad and his American buddies were glad to see the end of the war, not everyone was celebrating. There were enemy Japanese soldiers hiding out in the mountainous jungle who didn't even know that the war was over.

One day a group of sailors, including my father, talked their commander into giving them a day off to go to the beach. When they were told they could go, they piled into the back of a military truck for the trip to the ocean a few miles away. The commander then gave special instructions to the driver not to stop along the highway under any circumstances.

As they rumbled down the road through the jungle, my father lost his hat in the wind. He watched the hat as it floated to the ground, settling in the middle of the highway. The sailors began to yell at the driver asking him to stop while banging their fists on the roof of the truck to get his attention. Although they were making a great deal of noise, it seemed as if he could not hear them.

I am sure he heard them, but without pause he continued driving. Determined to obey orders, he would not stop for any reason. But before the truck rounded the next curve the sailors suddenly understood the reason for the commander's strict orders. Just a few seconds after the hat hit the ground, enemy Japanese soldiers came out of the jungle from both sides of the road. They picked up the hat and then disappeared back into the jungle.

The rest of the trip to the beach was somber and quiet as each young man thought about what had just happened. Seeing the potential consequences of disobedience reinforced the critical importance of obeying the commander's orders. The young sailors didn't calculate the risk when they chose to disobey. They had been willing to take a chance because they didn't understand the reasons behind the orders.

Isn't it the same with you and me? The understanding of Godly instruction can reinforce our ability to obey. And when you have the desire to understand, it is best to start at the beginning.

1

Who's Number One?

*"Loving-kindness and mercy,
truth and faithfulness, preserve the
king, and his throne is upheld
by the people's loyalty."*

PROVERBS 20:28 NIV

Chapter One

*E*ven before time began, there were contenders for God's throne. Lucifer was the first in his effort to oust God from His position. Although we don't know much about Lucifer's time in the heavens before he was cast down, we do know that he was the first source of rebellion.

Isaiah 14:12-14 tells us that he fell into pride and rebellion and declared, *"I will exalt my throne above the stars of God and I will be like the Most High."* NKJV

Lucifer was so full of himself that he left no room for God. His beauty was unmatched among the angels in heaven. He was covered in jewels which enabled him to literally reflect the glory of God. But this wasn't enough for him—he wanted more.

Lucifer's first mistake was believing that he was the source of beauty. He failed to realize that he was only beautiful when he was reflecting the glory of God. His own self-centeredness and pride blinded him to the fact that he could never be greater than the Lord God. In fact, *Lord* is translated from the Hebrew word *adown*, meaning, "sovereign" or "there is none above," and *God* is defined as, "the supreme or ultimate reality; the one who is worshiped as Creator and Ruler of the universe."

God could not tolerate an objection to His Lordship, so He responded to Lucifer's challenge. God commanded Michael, Chief of the warring angels saying, "Cast him out of heaven, and every angel that has anything to do with him."

ATTITUDE? WHAT ATTITUDE?

Although Lucifer was the first contender for God's throne, he was not the last. You see, the throne of God, or His place of rule, exists not only in the heavens, but also in the lives of His children. Sadly, God must now contend with our pride, greed and thirst for personal power. It is possible to exalt ourselves to the place of "lord" in our own lives and not even be aware of it. Yet this is the same spirit or attitude that caused Lucifer to lose his place in heaven.

If we allow it, this Luciferian attitude will challenge God's rightful position as Lord of our lives because it is in direct opposition to God. Remember, Lucifer's confession was, *"I will exalt my throne above the stars of God and I will be like the Most High."* (See Isaiah 14:13-14.) You can bet that when "I" comes first in our lives, trouble will most likely follow.

WHAT IS FIRST?

The office of Lordship and the station of the throne were created for the one true God. It is impossible for anyone or anything to replace God as first. With all this talk about the word "First," I may be taking for granted that we all have the same understanding of its meaning, which varies with it's occupation within a sentence.

FIRST, when used as a noun, is defined: **the first person or thing mentioned.** FIRST, when used as an adjective is defined: **being number one in a series, earliest in time, foremost in importance, rank; fundamental; rudimentary.**

The word *rudimentary,* as a synonym of first, is defined: **a basic principle of a subject, the merest beginning of something capable of being developed.** *Fundamental,* as a synonym of first, is defined: **a basic essential, affecting the foundations of something.**

So, if life were a sentence, God would be the noun. And how we chose to describe Him would be the adjective. Many of us would agree that He should be defined as the first person, in the sense that He was earliest in time and foremost in importance. However, we may never have considered defining Him as being number one in a series. It is essential that you understand this point before we go further with this subject.

One aspect of the definition of first, that has not clearly been brought out is that although *'first'* means number one, it does not mean that it is an island unto itself, having no effect on all that comes after. But instead, it is defined as the beginning or foundational principle. In other words, the foundation must always come first.

This principle is seen in design and construction. It would not take long to fail in the construction business if the contractor decided to start the building process with the walls or the ceiling. I know that may sound silly, but it wouldn't take a scientist to figure out that something is missing.

You see, the contractor could not ever successfully go beyond his first mistake. Without a foundation there is no question as to whether a building will fall, only when it will fall.

THE FALL OF MAN

When God created man, He created all things for his benefit. Adam and Eve were created to rule over all the earth. They were not created to be slaves to God, but to rule on His behalf as kings. All God asked of them was that they leave one selected tree alone. Adam and Eve were commanded not to touch it or eat it's fruit. God's intention was not to tempt them with the fruit of that tree, but to remind them that He was Lord. The tree of the knowledge of good and evil was to be a constant reminder that, although they had been given power and authority, they were still ruled by Another. Their first step toward falling was forgetting their Foundation.

In the garden, Adam and Eve had no knowledge of evil. Under the protection of God, they were not made vulnerable to the enemy. They knew the goodness of God, so the temptation to take what was God's held no real pleasure; it was simply a mirage. All that the serpent could offer them was the knowledge of evil and the pain that came with suffering. Because of the deception of the serpent, they disobeyed God and defiled themselves by partaking of what belonged to Him. The perception exists that there was something special about the fruit of that tree and that God had made it as tempting as possible because it thrilled Him to torture man. The truth is that the curse came to them because they neglected to put God and His commands first. Adam and Eve's desire "to be like God" ruled their ability to make a quality decision. Like Lucifer, their agenda took first place and set in motion the perpetuation of evil among man.

Far too often, our desires and plans are more important to us than God's. We can display a Luciferian attitude, challenging God's authority, if we follow our own agenda instead of God's plan for our lives.

In fact, in Luke 9:51-56, James and John were rebuked by Jesus for having this attitude. When the Samaritans refused to receive Jesus into their village, James and John asked Him if they could command fire to come down and consume the place. Jesus rebuked them by saying, *"You do not know what manner of spirit you are of. For the Son of Man did not come to destroy men's lives but to save them."* Luke 9:55-56 NKJV In other words, He was saying, "You and I aren't even on the same page. I didn't come to this world to destroy men—I came to save them!"

James and John thought they knew how the situation should be handled, but they didn't have the same objective as Jesus. Their agenda was to judge the people, while His objective was to save them. In the same way, you and I can be Luciferian in attitude, yet Christian by confession. Your confession may be, "Oh, I am a Christian. Jesus is Lord of my life," but your actions may reflect the spirit of Lucifer. You don't have to be demon-possessed to carry this spirit. It is manifested through an attitude or mind-set that sets itself above God.

God will not adjust His standard to our mind-set; we must adjust our thinking to His standard. Unfortunately, our thinking has become warped by the world in which we live. Our "bleeding heart" society is full of people who are willing to lay down their lives to save a tree, but choose to murder hundreds of babies every day with absolutely no conscience. The realization needs to occur that our society's standards are set by ungodly priorities and must be adjusted to God's principles.

WHAT ABOUT MY RIGHTS?

We live in a time in which we are obsessed with maintaining and expanding what we believe to be our rights. And as Christians, it is important to make a difference in our society by casting our vote. The problem is that some believers bring this attitude into the church and their relationship with God. However, as citizens in God's Kingdom, we have no spiritual 'rights' that over-ride the will and word of God. There is no political process, vote, or campaign in the Kingdom of God. God wouldn't be God if He ran things by public opinion polls and majority vote.

Even in the abundance of His grace and mercy, this principle remains -- If you don't give God first place, He will take it. He is God and He will not allow anyone to violate His rightful position.

Because God is sovereign, He has the right to make certain claims to our lives with which we aren't always comfortable. As Americans, we are at an extreme disadvantage in understanding Biblical relationship to God.

Do you know why?

Because we are one of the few people groups that have been raised with little or no understanding of a monarchy. When you live in a monarchy, you can't offer an opinion that usurps the opinion of the king. If you wish, you could march in the street proclaiming your rights, but the ruler of that kingdom, with the nod of his head, can have yours removed. In the same way, the Kingdom of God is not a democracy. He rules His Kingdom with absolute power and authority. And if we disagree— too bad!

Romans 3:4 says, *"Let God be true but every man a liar."* NKJV

This scripture makes the point very clearly— that if we disagree with God, we are violating the truth! You see, allowing violations to go unchecked would destroy the system that God has put in place for a purpose. This also holds true in creation. For instance, some people may say, "Look, it's not fair that the earth has to be the third planet from the sun. We want to be the first planet instead."

What would happen if it were possible to do such a thing? To say the least, it would upset the natural order of life on this planet. God positioned the earth where it is for a reason. Move it closer to the sun and we would cook--move it further away from the sun and we would freeze.

Sometimes an argument for fairness will result in unintended destruction. But we can rest in the fact that God's way is always right -- whether we agree or not. I wouldn't want my fate to be left in the incapable, immoral hands of the masses. Although I may not understand what He's doing, I prefer the safety of the hands of the Chief Shepherd.

As young pastors my wife, Kathy, and I were always excited to see new faces coming into our ministry. We were always grateful to welcome new members to our little church. Yet if a particular family decided that God was leading them away from our ministry, they seemed to carry our confidence right out the door with them. Because we were honored when they came to us, we automatically felt rejected when they left.

After God brought to light our mistaken perception, we realized how self-centered we were by thinking that HE, the Chief Shepherd, was unable to govern His own sheep.

It wasn't until we learned to trust God and love people unconditionally that our ministry flourished to the point where we couldn't keep count of all the new faces. Sure, it didn't seem fair to me when people that we had loved and pastored felt led to leave our ministry. However, now I know that just as sure as their identity couldn't be wrapped up in me as their pastor, my identity couldn't be wrapped up in the number of members in my congregation.

God was broadening my focus to include the greater picture, which would require my trust. It was during those times that I had to trust God and depend on my relationship with Him to resolve the unanswerable for me.

ABRAHAM AND ISAAC

When speaking of trust, the story of Abraham comes to mind. He knew nothing of God or Lordship when God called him. In fact, he was an idolater who didn't know, much less serve, the one true God. When we think about the patriarchs of the Bible, we tend to forget that most of them didn't begin their journeys as faithful followers of God. What then gave Abraham the courage to leave everything familiar to follow the voice of an unseen God? Can you imagine the level of trust it must have taken for Abraham to obey?

God had no personal relationship with man at this point in history. Abraham was the first man with whom God made a covenant. After the battle of the kings in Genesis 14, Melchizedek, King of Salem, blessed Abraham. And in turn, Abraham paid him a tithe, a tenth, of all the spoils of war with which God had prospered him.

This is the first mention in the Bible of a tithe being paid. So Abraham, before there was any requirement to do so, paid a tenth or tithe of his spoils to Melchizedek. Because Abraham recognized Melchizedek as the priest of the Most High God and gave the tithe, God recognized him as the "Father of the Faithful".

The result of Abraham's faithfulness was a wonderful promise from God. In Genesis 15:5, God brought Abraham outside of his tent one starry night and promised him a son whose descendants would be as countless as the stars above his head. Abraham was a 75 year old man when God gave him the promise, so it must have taken faith to believe it would come to pass. True to His Word, 25 years later, Isaac, the promised seed, was born to Abraham and Sarah.

EAGER OBEDIENCE

Years later, God came to Abraham and said, "I want you to meet me on a mountain I will show you, and sacrifice your only son unto Me." And yet, the Bible says that Abraham did not stagger at the promise of God. Even as difficult as this was, Abraham showed an eager obedience to do as God commanded. He rose early the next morning and took the donkey, the servants, and Isaac and began the journey toward the mountain God would show him.

It took them three days to get to Mt. Moriah. When they arrived, Abraham said to his servants, *"The lad and I will go yonder and worship."* Genesis 22:5 NKJV The word worship means, "to give reverence; to show worth to." Worship also denotes a showing of devotion. Abraham had devoted himself to God and was proving God's worth in his life by his willingness to sacrifice his only son.

So Isaac carried the wood for the sacrifice on his back. As they journeyed up the mountain, Isaac said to his father, "Dad, we have the wood for the sacrifice, you are carrying the knife and we have the flint to start the fire, but where is the lamb?" Abraham must have looked away for a moment to gather his thoughts. Then he turned to Isaac and spoke prophetically, *"God will provide Himself a lamb for a burnt offering."* Genesis 22:8 KJV

When they reached the top of the mountain, Isaac built the altar as he had seen his father do many times before. He assembled the stones and the wood while Abraham rested.

Then Isaac came and said, "Dad, I have the altar all ready. The wood is there and I've done it just like you have shown me so many times before, but where is the sacrifice?"

Abraham replied, "Isaac, you are the sacrifice." Puzzled by his father's response, Isaac questioned, "It's me? What do you mean, Dad? Remember all of the times that you took me outside the tent and told me about the night that God gave you the vision about the stars? Did God not give me to you, as the seed for a nation? I'm not even married. If I die, how will the promise be fulfilled?"

Abraham must have replied, "Son, I had the promise before I had you. So I trust God to know what He's doing. You are my firstborn, and the firstborn always belongs to God." So in obedience, Isaac submitted.

Abraham then approached Isaac as he lay on the altar. He took him by the hair and pulled his head back, just as he had done hundreds of times before with sheep. However, this was not a sheep—this was his son. The moment of truth had come when Abraham took the knife in his hand. As Abraham put the knife to Isaac's throat, the Angel of the Lord came and stayed his hand and said, *"Abraham, now I know that you fear God."* Genesis 22:12 NIV

The words, *"Now I know..."*, imply that at the bottom of the mountain, God questioned His place in Abraham's life. It was not until Abraham raised the knife to sacrifice his firstborn son that God knew His position in Abraham's life. You see, Abraham's faith consisted of more than empty words – it consisted of absolute obedience.

IMPOSSIBLE PROVISION

I have a dear pastor friend in Puerto Vallarta, Mexico, named Saul Gonzalez. I call him the "Apostle Peter" of Mexico. He is a man who is a passionate soul winner and church builder. The first time Saul invited me to speak in Puerto Vallarta, I witnessed a tremendous miracle of provision against impossible odds. Saul held regular services up and down the coast around Puerto Vallarta, but every few weeks he would rent a large hotel ballroom for a rally so that all of his members could be together in one place.

They were looking for property to purchase and build on but, because Puerto Vallarta had become one of the most popular vacation spots in the world, it seemed impossible for this small Mexican group of believers to compete with the high-dollar hotel industry. However, God had something else in mind.

When I finished speaking that evening, the musicians came and began to worship. There was tremendous brokenness throughout the congregation. As we worshiped, God dropped a prophetic word in my spirit. The Lord said, "Tell the people that because they have proven that I am first in their lives, I will provide them with property and two buildings. One will be a sanctuary and the other one will be used for training and education. These buildings will be completely paid for by one person and you will see it begin within ten days."

I shared this very specific word with Pastor Saul and he shared it with the people. Even though they had given sacrificially many times, their building fund was very small. How could this come to pass? Saul sat down after the service with his Elders and they all wrote the promise God had given them in the front cover of their Bibles.

The following week Saul flew to Dallas and walked into our mid-week service with the biggest smile I've ever seen and a testimony to go with it.

The night of the rally in Puerto Vallarta, a lady was in attendance whose husband is a developer of hotel properties. Three days after the prophecy, he called Saul to have lunch. After inquiring about the church building plans, he asked Saul to take a ride with him.

He took Saul to a beautiful city block of property and said, "Saul, I am not a Christian but I know when God is speaking to me. God has told me to build you a church on this property." Saul began to weep. He said, "Sir, if you can get us this beautiful property you could just put up some poles and a tin roof and we would be so grateful." The builder said, "Saul, have you seen my hotels? They have marble floors and crystal chandeliers. I will not build God a house with poles and a tin roof!"

I have been to Puerto Vallarta and preached in the new church building -- built and paid for by a man who had never been to a service.

God is able to provide what He promises!

Believing that God will do what He says becomes easier when we focus on God's promise instead of our sacrifice. If Abraham had focused on the sacrifice of his only son, he would have lost the promise of a nation. Had Abraham's choice been different, God would not have stopped loving Abraham, but he would never have become the "Father of many nations".

CHAPTER SUMMARY

- THE OFFICE OF LORDSHIP AND THE STATION OF THE THRONE WERE CREATED FOR THE ONE TRUE GOD.

- IT IS IMPOSSIBLE FOR ANYONE OR ANYTHING TO REPLACE GOD AS FIRST.

- LUCIFER WAS THE FIRST SOURCE OF REBELLION.

- THE LUCIFERIAN ATTITUDE WILL CHALLENGE GOD'S RIGHTFUL POSITION AS LORD OF OUR LIVES, BECAUSE IT IS IN DIRECT OPPOSITION TO GOD.

- ADAM AND EVE WERE NOT CREATED TO BE SLAVES TO GOD, BUT TO RULE ON HIS BEHALF AS KINGS.

- ADAM AND EVE DISOBEYED GOD AND DEFILED THEM-SELVES BY PARTAKING OF WHAT BELONGED TO HIM.

- THE CURSE CAME TO ADAM AND EVE BECAUSE THEY NEGLECTED TO PUT GOD AND HIS COMMANDS FIRST.

- GOD WILL NOT ADJUST HIS STANDARD TO OUR MIND-SET; WE MUST ADJUST OUR THINKING TO HIS STANDARD.

- BECAUSE GOD IS SOVEREIGN, HE HAS THE RIGHT TO MAKE CERTAIN CLAIMS TO OUR LIVES WITH WHICH WE AREN'T ALWAYS COMFORTABLE.

- AS CITIZENS IN GOD'S KINGDOM, WE HAVE NO SPIRITUAL 'RIGHTS' THAT OVER-RIDE THE WILL AND WORD OF GOD.

- SOMETIMES AN ARGUMENT FOR FAIRNESS WILL RESULT IN UNINTENDED DESTRUCTION.

- ABRAHAM WAS THE FIRST MAN WITH WHOM GOD MADE A COVENANT.

- ABRAHAM, BEFORE THERE WAS ANY REQUIREMENT TO DO SO, PAID A TENTH OR TITHE OF HIS SPOILS TO MELCHIZEDEK.

- ABRAHAM SHOWED AN EAGER OBEDIENCE TO DO AS GOD COMMANDED.

- THE RESULT OF ABRAHAM'S FAITHFULNESS WAS A WONDERFUL PROMISE FROM GOD.

- ABRAHAM'S FAITH CONSISTED OF MORE THAN EMPTY WORDS – IT CONSISTED OF ABSOLUTE OBEDIENCE.

- BELIEVING THAT GOD WILL DO WHAT HE SAYS BECOMES EASIER WHEN WE FOCUS ON GOD'S PROMISE INSTEAD OF OUR SACRIFICE.

2

Fulfilling The Promise

"I will multiply your descendants, as the stars of the heaven and as the sand which is on the seashore; and your descendants shall possess the gate of their enemies."

GENESIS 22:17 NKJV

Chapter Two

After Abraham passed the test of faith, the angel of the Lord appeared to him restating the promise using the words SAND and STARS to describe how numerous his descendants would become. Have you ever wondered why God used the word STARS?

Why couldn't God have simply said, "Abraham, you will have millions of descendants"?

Today, there are over six billion people on our planet, but in Abraham's day there were very few earthly inhabitants. So God, in His sensitivity to Abraham's lack of understanding, used familiar words to describe what He was promising. Abraham knew stars. At night, outside his tent, it must have seemed as if every cubit of the sky was frosted over with maximum star potential. Abraham also knew sand.

Although it would take faith to believe, Abraham could not receive the promise if he did not understand it. So, because there wasn't an abacus with enough beads to illustrate God's message, He found a way to make the promise relevant.

BECOMING A NATION

Isaac was the promised seed of the nation that was to come. Isaac, with his wife Rebecca, produced two sons. The firstborn of their twin boys was named Esau and the second-born they named Jacob. Esau's name, meaning "hairy", described his looks, however, Jacob's name meant "cheater", describing his character. Jacob was so named because he is said to have been holding onto his brother's ankle, vying for position, at the time of their birth.

Jacob became, for a time, exactly what his name meant, a cheater. And he too would be cheated by his father in-law out of the wife he so desired, Rachel. As a requirement of his father-in-law, he married Leah in order to gain Rachel. Jacob loathed the pattern that this name had brought him and feared it would be his end if God did not intervene to change him. After Jacob struggled with 'the Angel of the Lord' all night, God changed his name from "cheater" to Israel, which means; "prince who has power with God".

Jacob, or Israel, as he was renamed, eventually had twelve sons. The sons were named Reuben, Simeon, Levi, Judah, Issachar, Zebulun, Gad, Asher, Dan, Naphtali, Joseph and Benjamin, and their descendants became the 12 tribes of the nation of Israel. Of the 12 sons, Joseph was his father's favorite. Naturally, this aroused the envy of his brothers, who later sold him into slavery.

Most of us have heard of Joseph, or at least his famous coat of many colors, but many don't know the rest of the story that includes Joseph's imprisonment, slavery and reign in Egypt.

Joseph's long journey led him to the place of authority and honor he had seen in a vision as a young boy. Many years later, the same brothers that had sold him into slavery appeared before him in Egypt begging for assistance. As second in command, Joseph was able to provide valuable food and water for his father, his brothers and their families during the seven year drought.

Prophetically, Joseph had seen the coming of the famine and instructed the Egyptians to store up for its arrival. Joseph instructed his brothers to return to Canaan and bring his father to him to dwell under the shelter of Egypt until the drought was over.

Genesis 45:23 says, *"And this is what he sent back to his father ten donkeys loaded with the best things of Egypt, and ten female donkeys loaded with grain and bread and other provisions for his journey."* NIV

So, the children of Israel went into Egypt numbering 70, and stayed for four centuries. In the beginning, the children of Israel were received by the Egyptians. But not long after the reign of Joseph had passed, the children of Israel became a threat to the Egyptians because they quickly grew to out-number them. The Egyptians placed slave masters over them to oppress them with forced labor. But the more they were oppressed, the more they multiplied and spread; so the Egyptians came to dread the Israelites and worked them ruthlessly. The tactics of the Egyptians backfired because the children of Israel not only multiplied, but remained set apart due to their station as slaves. The children of Israel multiplied from 70 to roughly 2,000,000 people within 400 years. They had become a nation.

Now, when God was ready to bring the children of Israel out of Egypt, He picked Moses as the man for the job. Although Moses had been raised in Pharaoh's palace, he was born an Israelite. Moses, when he learned of his Israelite heritage, struck and killed an Egyptian who was beating an Israelite. With his true identity revealed and fearing for his life, Moses left Egypt. For 40 years *[which is the number of transition]*, Moses dwelt in the wilderness. God was making Moses into the leader He would use to deliver His people out of Egypt.

PLAGUED BY THE LAW

In Exodus 4:22, God instructed Moses, *"Then you shall say to Pharaoh, 'Thus says the Lord: Israel is My son, My firstborn. So I say to you, let My son go that he may serve Me. But if you refuse to let him go, indeed I will kill your son, your firstborn.'"* NKJV

In other words, God was saying, "Pharaoh, if you don't free My firstborn, Israel, to serve Me, then I am going to take your firstborn. Every one of them in the land." God was establishing a precedent when He instructed Moses to tell Pharaoh to let His firstborn go so that the firstborn may serve Him. He was ready to initiate His Law of First Things and His first course of action was to deliver His "firstborn". God considered Israel His firstborn because they were descendants of Isaac, the first-born son of Abraham, whom God promised to make a holy nation.

Pharaoh didn't respond positively to God's command. In fact, he refused to release the children of Israel. So God began to unleash plagues which became progressively more severe against the Egyptians in response to Pharaoh's defiance to His command.

The first plague was the turning of water to blood. Then came the plague of frogs, gnats, flies and the death of livestock. They began to get more severe by degrees until boils plagued the Egyptians and hail left the countryside in ruins to be eaten by the plague of locusts. Then, a darkness that could be felt spread over Egypt covering everything for three days. The Israelites, however, were spared and had light in the places where they lived. However, Pharaoh's heart only grew harder with each plague--until the tenth plague.

The tenth plague was the death of the firstborn. Every firstborn male of cattle and children died during the night. Remember that God sent Moses to Pharaoh with a message saying, "Let My first-born go to serve Me. If you don't, then I am going to kill your firstborn." Now isn't that what God said He would do in the beginning?

God wasn't vague in His command to Pharaoh. But look how merciful God is—God went through nine plagues before doing what He said He was going to do in the first place. See, each plague was more severe; but the Egyptians could have avoided the death of the firstborn after the first plague if they had said, "You know what, all of these flies are a sign from God. Someone's warning us that we are out of line."

The story of the plagues isn't a popular parallel that anyone would want to compare themselves with. Yet, like the Egyptians, there are those who feel like they are getting by because judgment hasn't fallen. Have you ever felt like someone was trying to tell you something? Maybe those little problems you are having in your life are God's warning plagues to say, "It's just a few flies and locusts now, but it's progressive. How far will it go until you realize that something is out of order?"

You may have lost your job—but you'll get another job. Or, maybe the old car just broke down—but it can be fixed. That's all it is—just a little trouble; but at some point you've got to ask, "Where is this leading?"

PASSOVER

Through the instruction given to Moses, God made a way of escape for anyone who would choose to obey. In Exodus chapter 12, Moses addresses the Israelites with the knowledge of how to properly redeem their household. He said that they must slay a lamb and cook the meat and eat the meat of that lamb with none to be left over. They were then to take a hyssop branch, and paint the doorposts, above and down the sides, and even the threshold, with the blood of that lamb.

Then Moses said in verse 23, *"When the Lord goes through the land to strike down the Egyptians, He will see the blood on the top and sides of the doorframe and will pass over that doorway, and He will not permit 'the destroyer' to enter your houses and strike you down."* NIV This is where the term *Passover* comes from.

The test of Lordship had been required of Abraham and would now be required of the Israelites. Their belief would be witnessed by all their friends and neighbors. If they believed and trusted, blood would coat the doorpost of their home. And if they did not believe, there would be a funeral soon after. God designed this test to separate the Israelites from the Egyptians, neighbor from neighbor, friend from friend.

At midnight, when the destroyer was released, if the blood of the lamb was applied to the post of their door the life of the firstborn of that house was spared or redeemed. Redeem means, "to buy back by replacing with an acceptable sacrifice."

Even though they had not been taught the concept of redemption, God used an unforgettable example to begin His teaching. He allowed them to redeem their firstborn with the blood of a lamb. And if they gave the price of a lamb, they were able to keep their firstborn and everything else in their house was redeemed.

Everyone who observed the law lived. And the firstborn of everyone who did not observe the law perished. I can only imagine what the newspaper headlines looked like in Egypt the next morning. The death toll must have been enormous. It says in Exodus 12:30, *"...there was loud wailing in Egypt, for there was not a house without someone dead."* NIV

Now, as cruel as this seems, I can still see the mercy of God in it because God used nine plagues to warn them. It was not an act of hostility by God but, in fact, a refusal by God to violate His own established law. When the Law of God is established it is non-discriminatory. You may or may not have faith in our judicial system, but when God is the Righteous Judge, then law is equally measured out. It works the same for everyone.

You may say, "But wait, maybe they didn't know about God's law." But you see, ignorance of God's law is no excuse for not keeping God's law. Pharaoh heard the Word of God and witnessed the evidence of His power but refused to comply. God could have done more to show His power, but He would not tip the scales to the point where no faith was required. God, in order to be God, had to keep the rules and the principles that He had established. He wanted the choice to be clear but not forced.

It is amazing that in this day and age people could claim ignorance of God. In fact, you would think that by now America must surely have reached a place where there is no excuse for anyone to be lost. The Gospel is broadcast on the airwaves and television and there are billboards and churches on every corner. And yet, there are still so many who sleep late on Sunday mornings and have absolutely no desire for the knowledge of the things of God.

The lesson of the plagues is this: If we fail to put God first, it does not stop God from being first. Like Pharaoh, we can claim there is no God but that doesn't challenge His Lordship at all. And it doesn't eliminate Him from being God.

If He is not first, then there is no redemption at work in our lives. And the unredeemed portions of our lives will become a curse to us. As we know, redemption means to buy back from and, in this case, it is to buy back from destruction.

EGYPT IN THE REAR-VIEW MIRROR

God delivered the children of Israel from bondage 430 years to the very day they had entered Egypt. Because of the destruction that came upon the Egyptians, the Israelites were driven out of the country in a hurry. So in the middle of the night, before their bread could rise, they left Egypt for freedom.

"Because the Lord kept vigil that night to bring them out of Egypt, on this night all the Israelites are to keep vigil to honor the Lord for the generations to come." Exodus 12:42 NIV

The Lord said to Moses, "This month is to be for you the first month of your year. Tell the whole community of Israel, that on the tenth day of the first month, each man is to take a lamb..... And on the fourteenth day, at twilight, slaughter it and consume it all."

So with this announcement from God, the feast of Passover was established so that none would forget how God had delivered them with a mighty hand.

THE LESSON OF THE LAMB

There are few things more touching than the love a child has for his favorite pet. And many times, the bond that is formed is one of the most significant in a child's early years. Many of us can remember a childhood pet that became a part of the family and was loved by all. God knew this would happen in every Israeli family. The Israeli children also had pets that they loved and took care of, but their pets were usually the sheep and other animals that were commonly raised by the Israelites. And He knew that when it came time to sacrifice a sheep that had become a pet, an explanation would be in order.

So, God said in Exodus 13:8, *"... and you shall tell your son in that day, saying, 'This is done because of what the Lord did for me when I came up from Egypt. It shall be as a sign to you on your hand and as a memorial between your eyes, that the Lord's law may be in your mouth; for with a strong hand the Lord has brought you out of Egypt.'"* NKJV

Now, when and why did He say for the fathers to explain the sacrifice ritual to their sons? We have to get practical with this. When an Israeli dad headed toward the pen to pick out a sheep and started toward the temple with his boy and the family pet, God knew the son was going to ask, "Why that sheep, Dad? That one is mine!" And the dad would say, "No, no son, that is the firstborn and the firstborn isn't yours. I know that you took great care in feeding it, and you were there when it was born and it is very special and, yes, you're the one that named it, that's true. But this one is the Lord's and this one goes to the temple. We do this because the Lord brought us out of Egypt with a mighty hand."

After this traumatic event, there would surely follow a barrage of questions about Egypt. Any child would want to know the details of such an event that could cost them their lamb so many years later. You see, the problem is that the son doesn't remember anything about Egypt—but his dad does. His dad remembers the beatings from Pharaoh's cruel taskmasters that left the scars on his back. He remembers what living in Egypt was like, but the boy has no way of knowing the horrors of slavery. Therefore, the ongoing sacrifice system was set in place by God so that His children would not lose touch with the memory of their past.

This story is an important lesson for the modern day parent. If you don't tell your children, they will never know what you have come through in your lifetime. So, unless you enlighten them, how will they experience the same gratitude for the great delivering power of God?

How many of you remember what Egypt was like? It would be beneficial to routinely give Egypt a backward glance, and then thank your Deliverer for a grand exodus from the old life of bondage.

CHAPTER SUMMARY

- THE CHILDREN OF ISRAEL WENT INTO EGYPT NUMBERING 70, AND STAYED FOR FOUR CENTURIES.

- THE CHILDREN OF ISRAEL BECAME A THREAT TO THE EGYPTIANS BECAUSE THEY QUICKLY GREW TO OUT-NUMBER THEM.

- WHEN GOD WAS READY TO BRING THE CHILDREN OF ISRAEL OUT OF EGYPT, HE PICKED MOSES AS THE MAN FOR THE JOB.

- GOD CONSIDERED ISRAEL HIS FIRSTBORN BECAUSE THEY WERE DESCENDANTS OF ISAAC, THE FIRSTBORN SON OF ABRAHAM, WHOM GOD PROMISED TO MAKE A HOLY NATION.

- PHARAOH DIDN'T RESPOND POSITIVELY TO GOD'S COMMAND TO RELEASE THE CHILDREN OF ISRAEL.

- SO GOD BEGAN TO UNLEASH PLAGUES WHICH BECAME PROGRESSIVELY MORE SEVERE AGAINST THE EGYPTIANS IN RESPONSE TO PHARAOH'S DEFIANCE TO HIS COMMAND.

- THE TENTH PLAGUE WAS THE DEATH OF THE FIRSTBORN.

- GOD WENT THROUGH NINE PLAGUES BEFORE DOING WHAT HE SAID HE WAS GOING TO DO IN THE FIRST PLACE.

- GOD MADE A WAY OF ESCAPE FOR ANYONE WHO WOULD CHOOSE TO OBEY.

- IF THE BLOOD OF THE LAMB WAS APPLIED TO THE POST OF THEIR DOOR, THE LIFE OF THE FIRSTBORN OF THAT HOUSE WAS SPARED OR REDEEMED.

- WHEN THE LAW OF GOD IS ESTABLISHED, IT IS NON-DISCRIMINATORY.

- IF WE FAIL TO PUT GOD FIRST, IT DOES NOT STOP GOD FROM BEING FIRST.

- PASSOVER WAS ESTABLISHED SO THAT NONE WOULD FORGET HOW GOD HAD DELIVERED THEM WITH A MIGHTY HAND.

3

Lordship Or Lipservice?

"But why do you call me Lord, Lord, and do not the things which I say?"

LUKE 6:46 NKJV

Chapter Three

PART-TIME LOVER

The children of Israel were His people and He was their God. He wasn't one of several gods, He was the only God. But more importantly, He was to be first. God was weary, however, with His children's temporary and sporadic commitments to firstness. Although they were devoted to Him during the hard times, at first opportunity they turned to unfaithfulness. God had just miraculously delivered them from the bondage of Egypt, yet He found them celebrating their deliverance with a golden calf.

Allow me to pose a question. Would you be willing to marry a person who said, "I love you. . .pretty much?" Or how about someone who said, "I'll be faithful to you for 360 days out of the year, but I'll need a vacation once a year for five days to do whatever I please—without accountability for my actions"?

I don't believe anyone would choose that kind of a relationship. And yet, we claim that Jesus is Lord, while only giving Him Christmas and Easter. Lordship will not work that way because the terms of the relationship are not being fulfilled. If He's not Lord of all, then He's not Lord at all.

LAYING DOWN THE LAW

Although God loved the Israelites, He was disappointed with them. He could not show Himself to them until they gave themselves wholly to Him. However, Moses knew God's nature and had such an intimate relationship with Him that God spoke with him openly.

The Bible says in Exodus 33:11, *"The Lord would speak to Moses face to face, as a man speaks with his friend."* In the passages following we can find an interesting conversation between God and Moses. Moses begins by saying, *"If You [God] are as pleased with me as You say, then teach me Your ways."* NIV

In the following pages, God explained how the Israelites could prove their desire for the leadership and Lordship of His accompanying presence. There, upon the mountain, God gave Moses the applications to fulfilling the requirement of calling Him Lord and receiving His favor.

It is important for us to understand that God wanted His people to be blessed, healthy and prosperous. Yet, for them to remain blessed something more than a yearly feast had to be established to ensure His position as Lord in their lives. He knew He couldn't leave Lordship to their emotions, memories or mood swings.

So along with the construction of the Tabernacle, God installed checks and balances in His system of Lordship to ensure that their confession was more than just words. By doing this, He established ways for His children to prove that He is first. The requirements were the Ten Commandments, the structure of the ritual of sacrifice, the statutes of the Tabernacle and what we now call The Law of First Things.

GOD'S LAW OF FIRST THINGS

The Law of First Things is the giving over as required, firstborn and first fruits as an offering in faith, proving the position held by God.

"The First offspring of every womb belongs to me, including all the firstborn males of your livestock, whether from herd or flock."

"Redeem the firstborn donkey with a lamb, but if you do not redeem it, break its neck. Redeem all your firstborn sons."

"No one is to appear before me empty handed."

"Bring the best of the first fruits of your soil to the house of the Lord your God."

Exodus 34:19-20, 26 NIV

And so, God established a system of sacrifice in which animals were to be burnt as an offering upon an altar. In Leviticus 1, God designated five animals as clean {acceptable} sacrifices, while declaring the rest unclean. So, there were two categories of firstborn animals: clean and unclean.

The clean sacrifices were oxen, goats, sheep, pigeons and turtledoves. It is also interesting that these same five animals were sacrificed by Abraham when God made covenant with him in Genesis 15. While the wealthy sacrificed oxen, the turtledove was the poor man's sacrifice. But because most of the Israelites raised sheep, the most common sacrifice was a lamb.

Now, the firstborn clean animal was considered to be an offering that was devoted to destruction or **'the devoted thing'**. *Devoted* means "the irrevocable giving over to the Lord, not to be taken back again " and *destroyed* means "to be consumed with fire as a sacrifice."

"But the firstborn of the animals, which should be the Lord's firstborn, no man shall dedicate; whether it is an ox or sheep, it is the Lord's. And if it is an unclean animal, then he shall redeem it...Nevertheless, no devoted offering...shall be sold or redeemed; every devoted offering is most holy to the Lord."

Leviticus 27:26-28 NKJV

The confusing part of the previous verse is the part about dedicating the firstborn clean animal. This simply means that firstborn clean animals could not be dedicated for any other type of sacrifice. They had to be destroyed by fire as a tithe offering, as it was not acceptable to dedicate a first-born lamb as a sin offering.

Also, God did not allow the substitution of a first-born clean animal. You could not redeem one clean with another, as that practice was reserved for the unclean. If it was firstborn and one of the five acceptable sacrifices—it had to die.

REDEEMING THE UNCLEAN

Although God's instructions regarding the sacrifice of the firstborn clean thing seemed straight forward enough, what was to be done with first-born animals that were considered unclean—such as a donkey? Remember the definition of 'redeem' is "to buy back by replacing with an acceptable substitute."

In Leviticus 27:27a, God gives us the answer –*"If it is an unclean animal, then he shall redeem it according to your valuation..."* NKJV

By redeeming something from God, we are acknowledging His claim on it by paying for it with an acceptable substitute. What if the Israelites had an unclean first animal but didn't have an acceptable substitute with which to redeem it? God addressed this issue in Exodus 13:13 which says, *"Every firstborn of a donkey you shall redeem by substituting for it a lamb, or if you will not redeem it, then you shall break its neck..."* AMPLIFIED

How could killing the donkey be more of a benefit to God's children than keeping it?

The firstborn donkey is God's and if for any reason it is not acknowledged as His, it becomes an open door for the devourer. By breaking the donkey's neck the Israelites were taking a stand against the curse and with their actions saying, "It is better to break its neck than to disobey God. If I do not give God what is rightfully His, I will bring a curse upon my life, and I cannot afford to do that."

In breaking the neck of the donkey, the owner would sustain the blessing of God and keep the protection against the devourer. If the firstborn donkey was not redeemed, it would bring a curse upon the household and cause more trouble than it was worth. God made it clear that by redeeming the unclean things with acceptable sacrifices, the Israelites would be spared the curse of destruction.

God didn't want human sacrifice. In fact, that was not a sacrifice He accepted. In Exodus 13:13b, God said, *"...and every firstborn among your sons shall you redeem."* AMPLIFIED

Under the Old Testament system of sacrifice, the firstborn son belonged to the Lord and in order to redeem the life of that child, a lamb was sacrificed. If this was not done, the child had to be dedicated to the Lord and left at the synagogue.

God required the first of everything. And if it wasn't the first, it did not even count as being given! To human reasoning, if I am raising 50, 100 or 1,000 sheep, and God requires one from me every Passover, why should it make a difference which one it is--as long as I bring Him a sheep. Why couldn't I bring him a big, fat woolly one or the one with the biggest horns or maybe the 4-H contest winner? God said, "I want the first one. I don't care if it's frail. The only defining adjective I care about is 'first'. The first are Mine!"

In reading this, you may be thinking: "Why is giving the first thing so important to the Lord?"

The Israelites probably had similar thoughts. "If He is Lord, He doesn't need my sheep! He doesn't need my kids! He doesn't need my money! He's Lord! He made it all!" That is true, but He put an automatic control mechanism in place as a reminder to us of what position He holds in our lives. He cannot fill any other place you choose to give him. It is impossible for God to become second or third. In fact, He says, "I'm not number eight—so don't bring me the eighth sheep! I'm Lord and that status deserves Number One! And if I'm not number one, I'm not even hanging out on your farm!"

If His portion is not first, blessing will not come to the rest of our lives.

I read an interesting article releasing the findings of a study conducted over a span of several years. A well-known institution followed 25 couples documenting the changes in each of their relationships. The study was formed to determine that the first three minutes of contact between the two partners would determine how the rest of the evening would progress.

At the conclusion of the study, each couple fell into one of the two categories. And to the institution's amazement, their research had been successful in determining the importance of the first few minutes of engagement between two partners.

If the couple had guarded their words, keeping the theme positive, the rest of their time together would follow suit. However, if they had started their first conversation out on the wrong foot, it was near impossibility to change the negative course of interaction.

It was found that the relationships that had failed to work had distinctly fallen into family dysfunction of one kind or another. The couples who had managed to make their first few minutes together a positive experience, were happy and remained together.

So, the study not only determined that the first three minutes changed the course of the evening, but that it also changed the final destination of the relationship. If the first portion was given to negativity, the outcome was negative and if the first portion was given to praise, the outcome was positive.

The Law of First Things dictates that whatever is done with the first determines what happens to all the rest. It works in any situation you apply it to.

THE HONEYMOON

During the time in the wilderness, God was

teaching the Israelites that He could not inhabit their lives and bless them if He was not First. He had found them, saved them, made covenant with them, and now desired to get to know them. God didn't intend this time in the desert to be torture: it was supposed to be a honeymoon for His people to get reacquainted with Him. So He gave them miracles, literally, every day. They ate miracle food; quail sometimes fell right out of the sky. Oceans stood on end. Rivers of water came out of a rock by either striking it or speaking to it. The Bible says that not one eye grew dim nor was anyone ill and their shoes and clothes were continually renewed. It was a honeymoon season. They were living in corporate blessing. God was restoring and preparing them.

And then at the end of 40 years, they came into the land which God had promised them many years before through Abraham.

CHAPTER SUMMARY

- GOD WAS WEARY WITH HIS CHILDREN'S TEMPORARY AND SPORADIC COMMITMENTS TO FIRSTNESS.

- GOD INSTALLED CHECKS AND BALANCES IN HIS SYSTEM OF LORDSHIP TO ENSURE THAT THEIR CONFESSION WAS MORE THAN JUST WORDS.

- GOD GAVE MOSES THE APPLICATIONS TO FULFILLING THE REQUIREMENT OF CALLING HIM LORD AND RECEIVING HIS FAVOR.

- THE ACCEPTABLE SACRIFICES WERE OXEN, GOATS, SHEEP, PIGEONS AND TURTLEDOVES.

- ALTHOUGH EVERY FIRSTBORN AND FIRST FRUITS WAS GOD'S, ONLY FIVE ANIMALS WERE ACTUALLY ACCEPTED AS SACRIFICES.

- IF THE FIRSTBORN - FIRST FRUITS WERE ONE OF THE FIVE ACCEPT ABLE SACRIFICES, IT HAD TO BE GIVEN TO GOD, AND COULD NOT BE REDEEMED.

- IF THE FIRSTBORN AND FIRST FRUITS WERE NOT ONE OF THE FIVE, IT STILL HAD TO BE ACKNOWLEDGED AS GOD'S BY REDEEMING IT WITH A SUBSTITUTE SACRIFICE FROM ONE OF THE FIVE ACCEPTABLE SACRIFICES.

- GIVING GOD THE FIRSTBORN BREAKS THE CURSE OF THE DESTROYER FROM ALL THAT REMAINS.

- KEEPING WHAT WAS GOD'S, BY EITHER NOT GIVING IT (CLEAN), OR NOT REDEEMING IT (UNCLEAN) ALLOWS THE CURSE OF THE DESTROYER INTO OUR LIVES.

- THE FIRSTBORN CLEAN ANIMAL WAS CONSIDERED TO BE AN OFFERING THAT WAS DEVOTED TO DESTRUCTION OR THE DEVOTED THING. DEVOTED MEANS "THE IRREVOCABLE GIVING OVER TO THE LORD, NOT TO BE TAKEN BACK AGAIN." AND DESTROYED MEANS "TO BE CONSUMED WITH FIRE AS A SACRIFICE."

- THOSE FIRSTBORN CLEAN ANIMALS COULD NOT BE DEDICATED FOR ANY OTHER TYPE OF SACRIFICE. THEY HAD TO BE DESTROYED BY FIRE AS A TITHE OFFERING, BY REDEEMING SOMETHING FROM GOD, WE ARE ACKNOWLEDGING HIS CLAIM ON IT BY PAYING FOR IT WITH AN ACCEPTABLE SUBSTITUTE.

- GOD REQUIRED THE FIRST OF EVERYTHING. AND IF IT WASN'T THE FIRST, IT DID NOT EVEN COUNT AS BEING GIVEN!

- THE LAW OF FIRST THINGS DICTATES THAT WHATEVER IS DONE WITH THE FIRST DETERMINES WHAT HAPPENS TO ALL THE REST.

- IF HIS PORTION IS NOT FIRST, BLESSING WILL NOT COME TO THE REST OF OUR LIVES.

4

When Will We Deal With Achan?

"...Achan, who brought trouble on Israel by violating the ban on taking devoted things."

1 CHRONICLES 2:7 NIV

THE CONQUEST OF CITIES

After 430 years in slavery and 40 years in the desert, it was finally time for the children of Israel to be established as a nation. God was going to rename them as He had Jacob. They were called "Hebrew slaves" and "Bedouins" because of the past they had endured. But that was about to change. If they were obedient, they would be known as, "The Children of the One True God," accompanied by all the benefits a good name has to offer.

So, with the future of His children in mind, God designed a plan that would cause other nations to shudder in fear at the thought of the Israelites. With Joshua as their leader, the Army of the Lord moved to the city of Jericho.

While the children of Israel encamped around Jericho waiting for the instruction from God, the people of Jericho, assuming they were under siege, tightly shut up the walls of the city.

" Now Jericho was securely shut up because of the chil-

dren of Israel; none went out, and none came in." Joshua 6:1 NKJV

While the inhabitants of Jericho waited, God spoke to His people through Joshua. God instructed them that Jericho would be the first city the Israelites would conquer. At this news, the children of Israel rejoiced because they knew that when God said this was the first then there were more to come.

God gave Israel detailed instructions about the battle of Jericho. For 16 verses in the book of Joshua, God told Israel how he would give the city to them. He made it very clear He was giving them Jericho. They would not have to strive, because He would fight the battle for them. All he required of them was corporate obedience and the city would be theirs.

You know the story. They marched around the city once a day for six days, and then seven times on the seventh day. Then on God's command they shouted in unity and the walls of Jericho fell inward on the city.

DON'T TOUCH THE DEVOTED THING

The Lord instructed them that Jericho was 'doomed for destruction'. They were not to touch anything within the city, but were commanded to burn it with fire. It is interesting to know that the root word *doomed* in the original language is the same word from which we get *devoted*.

In fact, in the original King James Version it says, "devoted to destruction." Because God had been teaching them about The Law of First Things, they understood the terminology. God was ensuring that everyone understood that this city was not theirs to keep, nor the wealth held within it. Because Jericho was first, it was 'the devoted thing'.

So, when it was time to carry out their instruction, what happened?

They marched around the city once a day for six days, and then seven times on the seventh day. And on the seventh day, just like He promised, the city of Jericho fell in on itself. The people of God were so full of faith! They had never taken a city before nor had they owned land. I can only imagine their excitement as they reflected on the promise that God was just beginning to fulfill.

The wealth of Jericho was amazing. There were bars of gold and shekels of silver stacked all along the streets by the inhabitants of Jericho who were planning their flight out of the city. The army of Israel was ordered to carry fiery torches and light everything until it was consumed. The gold and silver would be taken to build the temple, but no one could take of the wealth of Jericho for themselves.

Because everyone in the army of Israel understood the concept of 'the devoted thing', they believed the Lord and rejoiced in burning this city. Everyone in the Israeli army believed God's promise except a man named Achan. While they were sacking the city and preparing to burn it with fire as an offering to the Lord, Achan's faith failed. As the army ran through the city burning it with fire, he saw a stack of gold bars and silver coins and made a decision.

With no one close enough to see him, he wrapped his discovery in a Babylonian garment, put it on like a backpack and took it to his tent. That evening he dug a hole in the floor and buried his treasure there.

Achan knew he had sinned. How do we know? Because he hid what he had taken. If he was unaware of his disobedience, he would have taken his booty of war and flaunted it to his friends saying, "I did pretty good! Look what I'm going to take home to my family."

You see, customarily, the spoils of battle were given to the soldiers. Sometimes sharing in the riches of what they conquered was their only pay. But not this time--Jericho was 'the devoted thing'.

WHAT'S THE DEAL?

The next city God wanted to give Israel was a city called Ai. Now, compared to Jericho, Ai was a little hick town without a standing army. It was basically a wide spot in a camel trail. So Joshua told his army, "I don't even need to go. I will send a few of you to take that city." After the battle of Jericho, Joshua treated this like a simple, everyday errand. But there was nothing simple about the lesson God was prepared to teach His children.

As the Army of the children of Israel approached the city of Ai, their faith quickly faded. The men of Ai threw open the gates of the city and came running toward them with farm implements and sticks. It did not take long for the Israeli army to realize they were losing more than the battle. Men were dying. Something was wrong: losing wasn't part of the plan.

When the Israeli soldiers returned after running for their lives they said to Joshua, "Something is wrong. When God's blessing was on us, the city of Jericho fell in on itself and we didn't lose one man. But when we went up to take the little city of Ai, we lost 36 men! Tell us, what did we do wrong?

So Joshua fell on his face before God asking Him, "What's the deal?" And God said, "I'll tell you what the deal is. There is a thief among you and when you deal with that, my blessing will return."

It may seem harsh that God would risk the lives of His children because of the sin of one man, but God could not tolerate a violation of His law. We talk a lot about breaking laws, but is that really possible? Maybe with man-made laws, but not with God's. We don't ever really break a law; we violate laws and pay the consequences.

Let's use the law of gravity for an example. Have you ever seen anyone break the law of gravity? Would anyone dare say that they were attempting to break the law of gravity by throwing themselves from the highest building they could find? I don't think so, but why hasn't this been attempted?

Because the law of gravity cannot be broken. And it is common knowledge that when you violate the law of gravity it will have its consequence. It simply cannot be ignored.

Well, this may seem simple and obvious, but there are many people that confuse ignoring laws with breaking them. However, God has undeniably set in place natural and spiritual laws that have immediate repercussions for those who do not show a respect for them. When a spiritual law is violated, God's response is not determined by His emotion toward the incident or the person involved. His established laws apply equally to everyone and so must the consequences.

THE ACHAN FACTOR

So Joshua, understanding that they could not go on in violation of the law of God, made all of Israel accountable to the sin of one man. God had Joshua line up the whole nation, tribe by tribe. Interestingly, these tribes equaled the entire population of a major metroplex; about 3,000,000 people. The arduous process of bringing all twelve tribes of Israel before Joshua took all-day and part of another. All the while, God is allowing Achan to stand there, giving him the opportunity to confess.

We know that God eventually showed Joshua by a word of knowledge who it was. So, why didn't He lead him straight to Achan's tent in the beginning? He then could have taken Achan out and stoned him to death and it would have been over. But, instead, God gave Achan the opportunity to repent. What a witness of His mercy! There were several thousand people standing there and God was waiting for Achan. But, hoping to escape punishment, Achan stood in silence.

So, eventually Joshua narrowed his search and the other 11 tribes were dismissed. Achan must have been feeling the heat but continued standing, unrepentant. Joshua sorted through Achan's clan, then continued to his family until he was finally standing directly in front of Achan. Joshua looked into Achan's face, and he said, "Achan, give God the glory."

That seems like a strange greeting after such a long search. Yet it was more appropriate than any tongue lashing Joshua could have given. It was a simple conclusion. Achan had stolen the glory of God because he took of 'the devoted thing'. Joshua instructed Achan to go to the tent and dig up what he had taken and bring it before the people. And the Bible then says that Joshua gathered the army of Israel around Achan, his family, his animals and everything that he owned. Achan, his family and all his possessions were stoned until there was nothing left but a pile of stones and a trickle of blood.

Now, before you think this punishment was too harsh, remember this – God had just spent 40 years teaching Israel about the devoted things. Achan had the same understanding everybody else did. And besides, God gave him plenty of time to repent and confess.

See, by designating Jericho as a devoted thing, God was telling Israel that Jericho was just the first. If they believed God and obeyed, there would be more cities to come. Everybody understood the concept, believed God and obeyed - except Achan.

Because of one man's disobedience, the entire nation of Israel suffered the consequences. They had to deal with the Achan factor among them before they could come back under the blessing of God. And afterwards, Israel marched on, taking city after city – but only after they dealt with the thievery of 'the devoted thing'.

If we are family and we are one in the Lord, and if we are a body, like the scripture says, fitly joined together as a church, then my disobedience affects each one of you. This would explain why most churches are not under corporate blessing. In fact, while I know individuals who are blessed, I cannot name one church where everyone who comes under that ministry has more than enough.

When Israel was under corporate blessing in the wilderness, all of them ate manna; none of their clothing wore out; their shoes were renewed; their eyes were not dim and they were blessed--every one of them. Occasionally, we hear about a miracle of provision here and there. However, we seem to be content to have on one end of a pew a man who has made his first million, while at the other end of the pew there is a single mother who doesn't have food in the cupboard for tomorrow's meal.

The church is not under corporate blessing and I think it is because we aren't serious enough about the Achan factor among us. We must not look around to see who among us might be an Achan. The point is, there is a little bit of Achan in all of us.

We have become accustomed to the lack that surrounds us every day. It isn't unusual to pass a homeless person on our way home from work. We are used to believing that we all fend for ourselves and we need to take what we can get without expecting too much from life. Instead of running back to God when the devil steals, kills and destroys asking, "What's the deal?" we just say, "Well, that's life!" Ignorance of God's laws and unrepentant hearts have blinded so many believers to the blessing of God awaiting the destruction of Achan.

WAR OF ATTRITION

Many of us are in a war of attrition with the enemy. Are you willing to lose one child of your three in order that you may keep two?

How much are you willing to lose before you get on your face and say, "Father, what happened to Your blessing on my life?" How insensitive to loss have you become? How many teenagers are we willing to lose? How many families will we allow to be broken by divorce? How many business deals will go south before we recognize there is a problem? How much are you going to endure before you get on your knees and say, "God, where have I gone wrong?"

This may be news to you but, unlike us, the devil is not willing to lose anything without a fight. He is not willing to let you keep anything; he wants it all. He will claim what God has given you if he is given the chance. If you think the enemy doesn't remember what has been stolen from him, you will find this interesting.

When Yassar Arafat, the leader of the PLO, began to take cities, the first city he demanded was Jericho. Why would he demand Jericho? He may not even know why, because that land doesn't have much value, strategically or monetarily; in fact, it's really rather pitiful. But because a spirit of anti-Christ controls him, his possession of this city is an attempt to threaten God. Why? Because Jericho was the first city that God gave His people when they came out of bondage. So thousands of years later in response, Yassar Arafat said, "Jericho is the first city we want back."

If the devil wants all you have, why are you willing to let him take anything at all? He will not be satisfied until your life is in ruins and you are questioning the ability of God to provide. God's Law of First Things is your insurance that God will rebuke the destroyer and break the curse over your life. God instituted this Law for our benefit, but if it really works, does He Himself live by it?

CHAPTER SUMMARY

- GOD DESIGNED A PLAN THAT WOULD CAUSE OTHER NATIONS TO SHUDDER IN FEAR AT THE THOUGHT OF THE ISRAELITES.

- JERICHO WOULD BE THE FIRST CITY THE ISRAELITES WOULD CONQUER.

- THEY WERE NOT TO TOUCH ANYTHING WITHIN THE CITY, BUT WERE COMMANDED TO BURN IT WITH FIRE.

- BECAUSE JERICHO WAS FIRST, IT WAS 'THE DEVOTED THING'.

- EVERYONE IN THE ISRAELI ARMY BELIEVED GOD'S PROMISE EXCEPT A MAN NAMED ACHAN.

- ACHAN'S FAITH FAILED.

- THE NEXT CITY GOD WANTED TO GIVE ISRAEL WAS A CITY CALLED AI.

- IT DID NOT TAKE LONG FOR THE ISRAELI ARMY TO REALIZE THEY WERE LOSING MORE THAN THE BATTLE.

- GOD COULD NOT TOLERATE A VIOLATION OF HIS LAW.

- WE DON'T EVER REALLY BREAK A LAW; WE VIOLATE LAWS AND PAY THE CONSEQUENCES.

- GOD HAS UNDENIABLY SET IN PLACE NATURAL AND SPIRITUAL LAWS THAT HAVE IMMEDIATE REPERCUSSIONS FOR THOSE WHO DO NOT SHOW A RESPECT FOR THEM.

- BECAUSE OF ONE MAN'S DISOBEDIENCE, THE ENTIRE NATION OF ISRAEL SUFFERED THE CONSEQUENCES.

- ISRAEL MARCHED ON, TAKING CITY AFTER CITY – BUT ONLY AFTER THEY DEALT WITH THE THIEVERY OF 'THE DEVOTED THING'.

- GOD'S LAW OF FIRST THINGS IS YOUR INSURANCE THAT GOD WILL REBUKE THE DESTROYER AND BREAK THE CURSE OVER YOUR LIFE.

5

God Lives By His Own Law

*"For God has done what the Law could not
do, its power being weakened by the flesh.
Sending His own Son in the guise of sinful
flesh and as an offering for sin, God con-
demned sin in the flesh subdued, overcame, deprived it of its power over
all who accept that sacrifice.
So that the righteous and just requirement
of the Law might be fully met in us..,"*

ROMANS 8:3,4 AMPLIFIED

Chapter Five

God looked upon a world that He loved, that He created and people that He wanted to be in fellowship with. But there was an enemy ravaging them, devouring their understanding of Him. God made man with the freedom to choose Him on his own, but that had failed in the garden. Although He had a close relationship with a few men throughout the years, He had lost access to humanity, and humanity had lost access to Him.

God had not spoken through a prophet in over 400 years and the Ark of the Covenant had been misplaced. The Tabernacle and later the Temple were both just a meeting place for God and man. Yet, the people could only see the box, not the precious gift resting within it. The Israelites had become so enslaved to the walls, the ritual and the rules that they lost sight of the fulfillment. They were more concerned with the boundaries God had set for them than the opportunity for relationship available to them.

The Law of Moses, with it's sacrificial rituals, served as a constant reminder of the seriousness of sin. The sacrificial ritual had been unchanged since Israel had left the slavery of Egypt. Within the Law of Moses was the law of sin and death, which stated simply: Those guilty of sin must die.

But, because of His great love for His children, God allowed a clean animal to be sacrificed on behalf of the sinner. However, the sacrificial system was a temporary plan and it was falling apart. In the 400 years before Christ, the temple had been corrupted by the lust for wealth and power. The focus of sacrifice was no longer based on the pain of death associated with sin, but was focused instead on how much it would cost the sinner.

There were sacrifices of purification, peace and consecration. For purification, the daily offering of sacrifice had become the frequent form of covering sin. Any individual who had knowingly sinned could bring a sacrifice to the temple and receive atonement.

Sacrifices given for peace or consecration were voluntary, but were still conducted with much regularity. For centuries, the blood of bulls, goats and sheep had stained the altars and pooled on the ground beneath. Countless animals had been given as atoning sacrifices before God.

The law exacted a terrible price for the sins of Israel. But the purpose of the Law of Moses wasn't to give them a means of salvation, it was to teach them that they needed a Savior.

YOM KIPPUR—TO COVER

Although the Law provided for the atonement for their sinful nature as well as their trespasses, no one could perfectly recall every single act, thought or deed offensive to God. So for this reason, once a year, Yom Kippur—The Day of Atonement served as a corporate cleansing from these unintentional {ignorant} or unknown sins.

One of the rituals of Yom Kippur that made it different from the rest of the holy days, was the ceremony of the scapegoat. The priest would choose two goats. One would be chosen to die and the other to demonstrate the relinquishing of sin. Israel's crimes against God were ceremonially laid on the back of the scapegoat and then it was allowed to freely trot away into the desert. The other goat was placed on the altar and sacrificed to cover the sin of the scapegoat. This ceremony was a clear demonstration of the future coming of Christ.

Yom Kippur was a consuming ritual.

First, the priest would slay the animal and catch the first flow of blood in a cup. Moving into the Holy Place, the High Priest would then assume his duties at the table of showbread and the golden lampstand. The High Priest would lift the veil concealing the Most Holy Place and enter in. He would then move to the Ark of the Covenant and pour out the innocent blood onto the Mercy Seat. There the blood would cover the translucent gold lid, which contained the evidence of the sin of Israel.

All God could then see was the blood of an innocent lamb and not the sin of His people. Hence comes the term *Yom Kippur* which means, "to cover".

God would then push the judgment of sin forward one year until Yom Kippur returned. He did not push the sin forward, but only the judgment of it.

By postponing their judgment, He was giving man every opportunity to understand the love and desire He had for a true one-on-one relationship. God had given Israel the Ten Commandments to live by, but He knew He couldn't throw out ten rules and change the world. And because the Law of Moses made nothing perfect on it's own, He had to complete the original purpose of the Law, which was relationship.

So, it was time for God to produce a Redeemer.

BEHOLD THE LAMB

God had a Son—His firstborn and only begotten Son.

The Holy Spirit carried the Seed of God to the womb of Mary. Overshadowing her, she conceived. Jesus was born of a virgin and raised in wisdom and stature. Because Jesus didn't have an earthly father, He would bypass the genetic inheritance of iniquity. Therefore, unlike any other human, He was sinless.

When Jesus was a man of about 30 years, he

encountered His first cousin in the flesh, John the Baptist. John was baptizing in the Jordan River and Jesus went down to join the growing crowd of followers on the banks. I can picture Jesus with His arms folded, standing back with a big smile on His face. John the Baptist waded in the Jordan River about chest deep after finishing his message.

All of the sudden, a prophetic anointing came over John and he turned and pointed his finger and cried out to the crowd of people, *"Behold The Lamb of God who takes away the sin of the world!"* John 1:29 NKJV

These words were powerful. Jesus, a Lamb? The Lamb who taketh away the sin of the world? This was the greatest parallel ever drawn. There was so much about a lamb that Israel understood. They knew that firstborn lambs must be sacrificed. The firstborn lamb was a redemptive payment for that which wasn't acceptable to God. The lamb was the most common sacrifice, available to all. The lamb was the clean sacrifice by which anything could be redeemed.

I am sure that John the Baptist's words shocked and confused the on-lookers. Israel had long anticipated a king to rescue her, not a lamb to redeem her. They were wrestling with flesh and blood, hoping a mighty warrior would come to their physical world and lead them to political power. Yet, Jesus stated repeatedly that His kingdom was not of this world.

This also must have been confusing for the children of Israel. The Jews were content with their yearly sacrifice and empty traditions. They were simply unaware that the Law must be fulfilled. Israel did not know how badly they needed a Savior, a Redeemer—a Lamb.

God knew that Law without grace could not sustain humanity forever. He was withdrawing His blessing because of sin and the system of sacrifice was nearing its end. Jesus, as the Lamb, would erase the past and give grace for the future.

THE LAST DAY OF ATONEMENT

When John the Baptist by prophetic designation called Jesus a lamb, he sealed His fate. After 40 days in the desert, Jesus understood what He must endure and yet, He submitted. He could have refused His mission; after all He was flesh. He had a will of His own.

At times, the temptation to reject His calling must have seemed overwhelming, but He overcame by resigning His will to the Father. And Jesus retained the sinless nature of God that made Him a worthy sacrifice. After three years of powerful ministry, political and religious forces united in hatred to execute the Son of God. Although Jesus was innocent, He would die a horrible death usually reserved for thieves and murderers.

The Father had anticipated the pain and had begun to grieve long before the final Day of Atonement. Although fallen man had wounded and rejected Him many times before, nothing could prepare Him for the events ahead. The tearing at His heart was undeniable. He was God, but could not rescue. He was power, but He would hide His strength. Imagine the restraint needed to allow the torturous death of your only son.

I have a son, and there is nothing in the world I wouldn't do for him. Offering my precious son to be killed, as God offered His Son, is beyond my ability--I love him too much. But let's assume that I could somehow force myself to offer him. And just to make the analogy accurate, I would have to turn him over to a rebellious, hateful, reprobate mob to be insulted, rejected, abused, reviled, bloodied and beaten. And when they were through with that, he would suffer an agonizingly slow and humiliating death on a cross.

Compelled by my love for them, I would give all to pay for the chance to have a relationship with the members of that same rebellious hateful mob. Not a guarantee, not a promise, not a likelihood. Just for the chance.

The last Day of Atonement would prove to be the most powerful day in history. God's firstborn Son would become the sacrifice lamb and die for a dream.

The scripture says that during the torture and death of Jesus, God hid His face. Even while knowing the outcome, God did not neglect to feel the consequences of His decision to put us first. When they began the crucifixion process, both Romans and Jews, who had opened themselves to this, were manipulated by every demonic force belched out of hell.

The Bible says, *"And the Lord has laid on Him the iniquity of us all."* Isaiah 53:66 NKJV That means that the evil of every pedophile, every rapist, every murderer, every pervert that would ever walk the face of the earth was laid upon Jesus. Under demonic influence the crowds abused and beat Him. They ripped His beard out, they spit in His face and they bruised His body from head to toe.

Pilate, who was a cold-blooded Roman executioner, said, "I have never seen a man's face more marred than this man's. Behold the man, I don't even recognize Him. Look what you have done to Him." And yet, that was not enough. They took Him to a cross, stretched Him out and nailed Him there. They wounded Him, bruised Him more, cursed Him, and spat on Him again and again. Demons by the thousands rejoiced in an 18 hour, agonizing, torturous murder. And in the mean time—we walked away free and He died in our place.

So in type, we were the goat spanked on the backside and told to run toward freedom, while Jesus was slain on the altar for our sins.

JESUS THE HIGHPRIEST

In becoming flesh, Jesus made the impossible—reality. Since Jesus' time on earth, God had empathized more than ever about the frailty of flesh. Jesus, fully God, and fully man, would reconcile both. The last words Jesus spoke as a man showed He understood how God the Father felt about His children at that moment— *"Father, forgive them; for they know not what they do."* Luke 23:34 KJV

It's as if He said, "Father, I know You must hate what You are seeing, but remember why You sent Me. You sent Me because they don't know any better. We have a greater perspective and understanding. I am doing this to bring them to a place of right standing. When they are joint heirs, they will understand."

Not only was Jesus pleading our case, He excused our behavior. This was Jesus, our Great High Priest, making intercession for us even as He was dying. God was reminded of His word and the reasoning behind the act of sacrifice. Jesus, the Son of God, would take on the curse of the Law and allow Himself to die. God was willing to do whatever it took to restore us to full relationship with Him.

At the moment Jesus gave His life because of His love for us, there was nothing loveable about us. In fact, we were spitting in the face of the One who came to save us. But Jesus, full of compassion for His people, saw us for what we were and prized us for what we could become. He wanted communion with the family He created. The redemptive release of the lamb would make the possibility of that relationship a reality.

Could the fulfillment of the Law be more clear than this?

Jesus was the Lamb.

We were the scapegoat.

Jesus poured out His own blood as the High Priest.

Jesus' death and the method by which it took place fulfilled the Law. This is what Jesus meant when He said, *"Do not think that I came to destroy the Law or the Prophets; I did not come to destroy, but to fulfill."* Matthew 5:17 NKJV

If we take what we have learned about redeeming the unclean with the clean, the lesson of the Law is clear. If the clean is first given, then all that comes thereafter is redeemed. We were the unclean, so the Father sent a clean, spotless, sacrifice. Because the clean animal, firstborn, cannot be redeemed, but has to die, Jesus the clean, redeemed humanity, the unclean. Jesus was freely given as 'the devoted thing'.

God never asks us to follow His established laws of the earth without being completely committed Himself. His Law in Leviticus required the giving of the first born lamb. So, in order to fulfill the Law, God was required to sacrifice His only Son. That example answered the question asked by generations of Israeli children - "Dad, why are we doing this?"

God was serious about The Law of First Things then, and He still is. If God had not been, then He would have ignored it when it came to His only Son, Jesus-- but He did not.

So does God live by His own law?

He does.

God has not asked us to do something that He has not done Himself. God prepared Himself a sacrifice…. and His sacrifice was the ultimate expression of love for His people.

Putting us first, He would give whatever He had to be first in our lives.

WHEN GOD IS FIRST

CHAPTER SUMMARY

- BECAUSE OF SIN, GOD HAD LOST ACCESS TO HUMANITY, AND HUMANITY HAD LOST ACCESS TO HIM.

- THE ISRAELITES WERE MORE CONCERNED WITH THE BOUNDARIES GOD HAD SET FOR THEM THAN THE OPPORTUNITY FOR RELATIONSHIP AVAILABLE TO THEM.

- THE FOCUS OF SACRIFICE WAS NO LONGER BASED ON THE PAIN OF DEATH ASSOCIATED WITH SIN, BUT WAS FOCUSED INSTEAD ON HOW MUCH IT WOULD COST THE SINNER.

- THE PURPOSE OF THE LAW OF MOSES WASN'T TO GIVE THEM A MEANS OF SALVATION, IT WAS TO TEACH THEM THEY NEEDED A SAVIOR.

- YOM KIPPUR—THE DAY OF ATONEMENT SERVED AS A CORPORATE CLEANSING FROM THESE UNINTENTIONAL {IGNORANT} OR UNKNOWN SINS.

- YOM KIPPUR MEANS, "TO COVER".

- GOD WOULD THEN PUSH THE JUDGMENT OF SIN FORWARD ONE YEAR, UNTIL YOM KIPPUR RETURNED.

- BECAUSE JESUS DIDN'T HAVE AN EARTHLY FATHER, HE WOULD BYPASS THE GENETIC INHERITANCE OF INIQUITY.

- WHEN JOHN THE BAPTIST BY PROPHETIC DESIGNATION CALLED JESUS A LAMB, HE SEALED HIS FATE.

- JESUS RETAINED THE SINLESS NATURE OF GOD THAT MADE HIM A WORTHY SACRIFICE.

- THE LAST DAY OF ATONEMENT WOULD PROVE TO BE THE MOST POWERFUL DAY IN HISTORY. GOD'S FIRST BORN SON WOULD BECOME THE SACRIFICE LAMB AND DIE FOR A DREAM.

- JESUS, THE SON OF GOD, WOULD TAKE ON THE CURSE OF THE LAW AND ALLOW HIMSELF TO DIE.

- JESUS' DEATH AND THE METHOD BY WHICH IT TOOK PLACE FULFILLED THE LAW.

- JESUS THE CLEAN, REDEEMED HUMANITY, THE UNCLEAN.

- JESUS WAS FREELY GIVEN AS 'THE DEVOTED THING'.

- GOD NEVER ASKS US TO FOLLOW HIS ESTABLISHED LAWS OF THE EARTH WITHOUT BEING COMPLETELY COMMITTED HIMSELF.

- GOD PREPARED HIMSELF A SACRIFICE.

6

Qualified To Be Multiplied

"...unless a grain of wheat falls into
the earth and dies, it remains
one grain: it never becomes more,
but lives by itself alone.
But, if it dies, it produces many others,
and yields a rich harvest."

JOHN 12:24 AMPLIFIED

Chapter Six

In 1990, my son Stephen and I went for a drive to take a look at a piece of property for sale. We had outgrown the church building that had been continually added on to since we built it in 1980. The neighborhood had grown up around us and we found ourselves out of options and out of pews. So I knew I'd better check out this opportunity.

Stephen jumped up in my truck and we headed a couple miles east toward the Dallas tollway. As we approached the open plot of land, I wondered how many times that I had passed it without the consideration of one day building on it. It was 22 prime acres of undeveloped land directly in the center of new development. As Stephen and I got out to take a walk around, he asked me a profoundly simple question that probed my thoughts for a much deeper answer.

"Dad, how long has this land been here?" he asked.

As I turned to face him, I was unsure of how to

answer until the words came. "Well Stephen, I guess God's been saving it for us since creation," I said. And after a little more thought I started to realize just how true that was.

Not too long before, my wife Kathy had received a fascinating old newspaper article about a woman born August 23, 1858 in what is now Carrollton, Texas. It read as follows:

"You wouldn't think Aunt Nanny McCormick of Carrollton is 99 years old..."

"Back in 1915, the men-folk didn't think they could afford to replace the log cabin Baptist church in Hebron which Aunt Nanny had helped establish 32 years earlier. But, that was before she had set her mind to a new building, with Mrs. Gus Marcy driving her over hill and vale in a rickety early day auto, to solicit funds."

"Harry Lord, who still lives in Carrollton, was running the Hebron gin. Aunt Nanny walked in and told them of the new church plan and it didn't set well. So she closed the door and said, "Let's talk to the Lord about it.""

"By the time she got through prodding them with real prayer, Uncle Bob Curtis gave the land for the new building, and the whole shebang was converted."

"She and her husband, the late Uncle Bud McCormick, gave all their savings to complete the structure, which still stands. They had pinched their pennies for a new home but sacrificed the savings. Since then, she calls the church her home."

"The pert little lady, whose hair still hadn't wholly whitened, is amazingly alert, looking forward to her 100th birthday. She recalls the days when she organized the church to begin services in 1883, with humor. "We didn't pay the preacher in money. Just hams, sausage, flour, and syrup and stuff, " she recalls. "Onc time a preacher mentioned to a member that the syrup he'd got was awful thin, and the member told him that the preaching had been pretty thin, too."

"Her keen memory and wit are sharpened by endless events, which she recalls with clarity. And the lives of her fore-bearers are steeped in contribution to the parade of pioneers."

(TIMES HERALD DECEMBER 1957)

Kathy and I became fascinated with this woman, referred to as "Aunt Nanny', who had lived a century earlier. This article was more than just interesting to us. The landmarks in that article were easily recognizable as we lived within a few miles of them.

You see, God had sent us to Carrollton to build a church in 1976. At the time, we didn't know of any ancestry in the entire metro area, let alone Carrollton. But God had given us a burden for this city, and the article about Aunt Nanny was the key to learning why we were here.

You see, we found out Aunt Nanny was my wife's great, great-aunt.

Afterwards, my wife said, "Mike, do you think we really had anything to do with coming to this city?" We both had one of those moments when you see the plan God is accomplishing through you. Seeing the hand of God, and His willingness to answer prayer, simply overwhelmed us.

And because of one woman's desire to see a church built for the glory of God, a spiritual seed was planted in the city of Carrollton that would continue to bear fruit for generations.

Today our church owns over 40 acres of land and has built $20,000,000 buildings to the glory of God. Although we are seeing the manifestation of a vision, it didn't begin with us. It didn't even begin with Aunt Nanny. It really began at creation.

When we, as God's people, begin to see history as the implementation of God's plan in the earth, and not simply as a sequence of random events, then we will begin to learn the heart of God. And more importantly, understand His purpose.

LEARNING BY COMPARISON

The similarities between the story of Abraham and Isaac and the story of God and Jesus are not coincidental. Abraham's sacrifice was foreshadowing God's ultimate expression of The Law of First Things. Abraham and Isaac were an example of the plan to come. Let's examine the similarities.

A promise to produce a nation.

A promise to produce a kingdom.

An agonizing father that lived by the first
things law.

An agonizing Father that lived by His own law.

An obedient son, willingly climbed upon
the altar.

An obedient Son, willingly hung upon a cross.

On a hill called Moriah, the sacrifice was
provided for the son.

On a hill now called Golgatha, the sacrifice *was*
the Son.

Same hill. Same principle. Distinctly different.

One victory declared submission to Lordship.

One victory declared He is Lord.

IN YOUR HEART OR IN YOUR HAND

Isaac was the down payment, the deposit, of the
original promise God had given Abraham. The
temptation facing Abraham, however, was becoming so overwhelmed with love for his only son that
he could forget the promise was for an entire
nation. Although Abraham was a man who trusted
God, he must have wondered at God's request to
sacrifice Isaac before Isaac had any children.
Wouldn't this short-circuit the whole promise?

What would have happened if Abraham had
decided to keep Isaac? I believe God would have
said "Okay, Abraham, I gave him to you, and if you

want to keep him, he's yours. But remember, the promise wasn't for one boy, but for a nation. And if you want to keep the one boy, he's yours to keep. But your family will live and die and never go further than your tent, because your son- your first-born son- is the seed. Isaac may live a long time, but he will be a seed unredeemed, and I make no plans for unredeemed seed. But if you will lay him down, I will raise him up. He will be redeemed because he is mine and I will build a nation from him. And everything that comes afterwards will be anointed and blessed because you gave the first-born to me."

If you ever lose sight of the promise of God, you will be tempted, as Achan was, to grab the tangible 'now' in lieu of the future promise. Abraham had to release what was in his hand if he wanted to receive the promise of God that was in his heart. And this is the situation many of us are in today. Abraham knew the promise was not for one son, but for a nation! He had to be willing to offer the son if he wanted the nation that was promised long before he had the son.

RESURRECTED IN POWER

When Isaac was laid on the altar, God said, "Raise him up." When Jesus was laid down as the clean offering sacrifice, God was obliged to raise Him up, because First Things given are never lost.

You may ask, "Did Jesus really die?" Sure He did, but there was a resurrection. The Word says,

"...unless a grain of wheat falls into the earth and dies, it remains one grain: it never becomes more, but lives by itself alone. But, if it dies, it produces many others, and yields a rich harvest." {John 12:24} AMPLIFIED

Even in nature, every time a seed falls to the ground, what do you think has to happen for that seed to germinate and become a living plant that can produce a harvest? It has to die! In the death process, the husk breaks open and the germ of life bursts out of the shell and produces new life.

You don't ever lose what is given to God! He is a Creator, not a consumer. When you give to God there is a multiplication of the seed—a resurrection. And there is always a resurrection in God! You see, God can raise the dead, but He cannot redeem that which has not been given. After being given to God as the firstborn, Isaac was 'resurrected' in power to fulfill his God-given purpose. By faith, Abraham had given Isaac to God, becoming qualified to be multiplied through Isaac, thus fulfilling the promise God had given him.

Now what was the next major event in Isaac's life?

Abraham called in his chief servant and asked him to go and find a wife for Isaac. Abraham sent the servant with ten camels loaded with gifts for Isaac's future bride. Why ten camels? Because ten is the number for redemption.

Since Isaac had been given to God, he was the redeemed seed. The ten camels symbolized the redemptive work of God, but that work could only happen after Abraham had given Isaac, in faith, as the firstborn offering.

Just like He asked Abraham to give Isaac when Abraham had no other children, God gave Jesus with nothing but a promise that if Jesus would be given, there would be more to come thereafter. Jesus would be the redemptive offering. The Church of the Lord Jesus Christ is the fulfillment of that promise. God is waiting for His Bride and He has sent redemption to us loaded down with a promise of our future.

If Isaac was the down payment of the blessing that followed Israel if they walked in obedience, how much more blessing should we expect if Jesus was the down payment for our New Covenant?

It is no coincidence that God has raised up Covenant Church from the same soil in which Aunt Nanny planted a seed. I'm sure she didn't know she was planting a seed and that what she was birthing would continue long after her death. In fact, Aunt Nanny had taken pride in the parade of pioneers and fore-bearers from which she had come. She probably thought that she was the fruition of many years of prayer and sacrifice, and she was. But in planting her sacrifice she became the perpetuation. But that's the way seed works, even in the spiritual realm.

After the sacrifice is laid on the altar, God will faithfully resurrect it. Only then, do you become qualified to be multiplied.

CHAPTER SUMMARY

- WHEN WE, AS GOD'S PEOPLE, BEGIN TO SEE HISTORY AS THE IMPLEMENTATION OF GOD'S PLAN IN THE EARTH, AND NOT SIMPLY AS A SEQUENCE OF RANDOM EVENTS, THEN WE WILL BEGIN TO LEARN THE HEART OF GOD. AND MORE IMPORTANTLY, UNDERSTAND HIS PURPOSE.

- IF YOU EVER LOSE SIGHT OF THE PROMISE OF GOD, YOU WILL BE TEMPTED, AS ACHAN WAS, TO GRAB THE TANGIBLE 'NOW' IN LIEU OF THE FUTURE PROMISE.

- WHEN JESUS WAS LAID DOWN AS THE CLEAN OFFERING SACRIFICE, GOD WAS OBLIGED TO RAISE HIM UP, BECAUSE FIRST THINGS GIVEN ARE NEVER LOST.

- GOD IS A CREATOR, NOT A CONSUMER.

- BY FAITH, ABRAHAM HAD GIVEN ISAAC TO GOD, BECOMING QUALIFIED TO BE MULTIPLIED THROUGH ISAAC, THUS FULFILLING THE PROMISE GOD HAD GIVEN HIM.

- GOD IS WAITING FOR HIS BRIDE AND HE HAS SENT REDEMPTION TO US LOADED DOWN WITH A PROMISE OF OUR FUTURE.

- AFTER THE SACRIFICE IS LAID ON THE ALTAR, GOD WILL FAITHFULLY RESURRECT IT. ONLY THEN, DO YOU BECOME QUALIFIED TO BE MULTIPLIED.

7

The New Covenant —
A better Plan

*"For the Law of the Spirit of life which is
in Christ Jesus, has freed me from the
Law of Sin and Death."*

ROMANS 8:2 AMPLIFIED

We saw that when Israel obeyed God by obeying the Law of First Things, the destroyer was rebuked and they were blessed. For 40 years Israel enjoyed national corporate blessing in the wilderness when they obeyed. God gave them complete provision and perfect health. Although they marched in total victory when they put God first, we also learned that disobedience, like Achan's, brought destruction by removing God's protective blessing. Now, what does this have to with us? All of those Old Testament laws, commandments, and promises were done away with at the cross, right?

THE DEATH OF A SYSTEM

Jesus was sacrificed as God's Passover lamb because God was providing a way for the redemption of His creation. Israel slew their lambs on their thresholds on the eve of their redemption from Egypt, but Jesus was sacrificed on the threshold of a new era.

In Egypt, the lamb's blood was splashed on the doorposts, but the blood of Jesus was splashed on every generation, past, present, and future. Jesus' sacrifice was the bridge between the old system and the New Covenant.

Many people are confused about what exactly was crucified with Christ. Some think everything related to the Old Testament, every law and commandment was done away with, but that isn't true. The Ten Commandments will still provide blessing to anyone trying to live by them.

God never intended to do away with the Law itself. His intent was to change our natures so that the spirit of the Law was written in our hearts and minds.

What died with Jesus was the curse of the Law of Sin and Death. Sin no longer requires death for redemption. Jesus died once for all, and if the destroyer sees the blood of Jesus applied to your life, he must pass over you!

FROM SHEEP TO SHEKELS

So how do we obey God's Law of First Things today? Does tithing, the giving of the first tenth of our increase, apply to us? Let's review what we have already learned.

We know that God, as a reminder of His Lordship, commanded the people of Israel to give the First Things. Remember the foundational principle: The first things - children, animals, crops, fruit of the tree...whatever - were to be given to God. God said, "I want the first portion of everything."

When Israel was a nation of farmers and shepherds, everyone owned land and livestock. Therefore, determining the first thing was easy because it was the firstborn or first fruits. However, God knew that the livestock-and-crops economy would gradually evolve to a monetary system. Thus, God had to make a way for the giving of first things in a cash economy.

So, "OK God, if it is money, how much should it be?" Well, if it is a redemptive work, guess what God would say? He said, "Let it be the tenth part." That is where the 10% tithe came from. In fact, the word *tithe* means 'tenth'.

"And all the tithe of the land, whether of the seed of the land or of the fruit of the tree, is the Lord's; it is holy to the Lord."

Leviticus 27:30 AMPLIFIED

If the tithe means a tenth, why a tenth? Because, ten in the scripture is always the number for redemption.

Ten Camels-for Isaac's wife, Rebecca.

Ten Donkeys-sent to bring Israel to Egypt.

Ten Plagues-used to free the Israelites from Egypt.

Ten Commandments-for the Israelites to obey.

Anytime there is a redemptive work in progress, there will be a number ten involved. So there were ten plagues and then the children of Israel were redeemed out of Egypt. There were Ten Commandments, and God said, "If you will obey these ten things, I will redeem you."

How many of you understand that God could have thought of more than ten things to require of His people. But, every time ten is used, God is working to buy back that which He desires.

If the tenth is a type of redemption, then why must it be first? Because when it's given first it breaks the curse of destruction off of the remaining 90%, releasing it to be used for its best purpose!

TITHING OR TIPPING GOD?

It is possible to be giving ten percent of your income and not be tithing; therefore, and so the blessing of the tithe is not on that which remains. If it is not first, it is only an offering. God will bless offerings, but the redemptive blessing is reserved for the first portion.

Recently, I was a guest minister on The Trinity Broadcasting Network. Jesse Duplantis, an evangelist from New Orleans, was hosting the program. After sharing some of the teaching about "First Things," I demonstrated my point by laying ten gold coins in a row on the coffee table in front of us on the set.

While pointing to the coins, I said to Jesse and the audience, "I would like to ask two questions in light of the truths I have just shared. First, if these coins represented my income this week, how many coins do I owe God as my tithe?" Jesse answered, "One!" I said, "Okay now, every Christian in the world knows that, but the revelation is contained in the answer to the next question. Which coin represents my tithe?" Jesse laughed and said, "I'm not sure I should answer that!" The audience was shouting, "The first one!" They got it!! The first one is the only one that carries the power of redemption. All of the remaining coins are "redeemed" because of what is done with the first one.

Since the night of that telecast, I have found that there is a third question that we must answer. How do we know which coin is the first one? The answer is that it is the first one spent!

See, the test of Lordship does not wait until you have all of your retirement arranged, your insurance current, your cars paid off, a little bit of a nest egg put back so that then you can say, "Now I will give God a little tip!"

Tithe is given *first* in faith to guarantee God that He deserves first place because of who He is, not what He provides. It may be ten percent but if it is not the first fruits it doesn't count as tithe, it is just an offering. Most offerings are an afterthought brought on by an inspiring word or blessing from God. Don't get me wrong, offerings are beneficial to the work of the ministry but are not meant to establish Lordship.

Let's look at the example of the first offering ever recorded. In Genesis 4:2-7, we can examine the difference in God's response to those who determine to put Him first and those who do not.

"Now Abel kept flocks, and Cain worked the soil. And in the course of time Cain brought to the Lord an offering of some of the fruit of the ground. And Abel brought of the FIRSTBORN of his flock and of the fat portions. And the Lord had respect and regard for Abel and his offering, but for Cain and his offering, He had no respect or regard. So, Cain was exceedingly angry and indignant, and he looked sad and depressed. And the Lord said to Cain, 'Why are you so angry? And why do you look sad, and depressed and dejected? If you do what is right, will you not be accepted? But if you do not do what is right, sin is crouching at your door: it desires to have you, but you must master it.'" KJV/NIV

When you understand the Law of First Things, the story of Cain and Abel is so much more interesting. It is evident that Cain's infamous anger was triggered by the lack of acceptance from God. But why was God unwilling to release blessing upon him? Let's examine what the story was truly about— their method of giving.

Abel brought an offering of the *firstborn*, but Cain brought only an offering of *some* of his increase! And God blessed Abel and warned Cain.

Cain was clearly disobeying – God said, "If you do what is right, will you not be accepted?"

What was the difference between the two? Abel's offering was the first portion, Cain's was not. Abel put God first, Cain did not. Cain did not make Him Lord, and therefore he was vulnerable to sin.

What God was emphasizing in this example is this: the order of that which is given to Him clearly defines His place in your life. He does not need what we are giving! He is God! He owns the cattle of a thousand hills. He had it before you earned it, and He'll have it after you're done with it. What He does need is the First, because that is the position reserved for Him.

When the first is given, it buys back (or redeems) all that remains from the curse of destruction. God's Law of First Things is created for our benefit. However, if we disobey and keep what belongs to Him, the first things become a curse to us. Did you know God called 'the devoted thing' 'accursed' if we withhold it? Remember that God said, "If you don't redeem your firstborn donkey, then break its neck. If you ride my donkey, unredeemed, it will become a curse to you." He never intended for us to bring the curse upon ourselves.

It is not an issue of heaven or hell. It is an issue of success or failure. When we put the Lord first, He stops the power of the destroyer in our lives. And more importantly, we prove not only to God His importance in our lives, but we reinforce that in our own minds.

I recently shared the "First Things" message for one of my good friends who pastors in the Midwest. His church is an exciting group of people involved in an aggressive vision to reach their city. A young man in the congregation who plays professional football heard the message.

After the service he came to the pastor's office moved to tears. "Pastor," he said, " I need to repent, I didn't know about The Law of First Things. Last week I signed a new contract with the team and received a large signing bonus. I'm just a farm boy with simple tastes but before doing anything I bought a ring for my wife and a Corvette for myself. I didn't give God the first fruits and I'm sorry. Here is a check for my tithe and my promise that I will never fail to put God first again."

My friend rejoiced to receive one of the largest tithe checks his church had ever been given. And better still, this young man has become one of the highest paid players in his position in the NFL. He never fails to give his first fruits tithe to the Lord. In fact, if he is playing out of town, he actually mails his tithe overnight to his church. God is faithful to bless those who put Him first. And He will forgive those who have failed to put Him first in the past.

REBUKE THE DEVOURER

It is in keeping what belongs to God and denying the provision and protection of Lordship that is the curse. Our disobedience provides an open door for demonic destruction. At the end of life, most people do not have enough money left over to cover burial expenses.

So, throughout their life what has been done with the money they controlled? Where did it go? Haggai 1:6 says that for all your striving to take care of yourself and all of your needs, you have earned wages and put them in a bag with holes in it.

This is the same scenario that I faced in counseling with the young couple I mentioned in the introduction. They were open to the devourer and their provisions seemed to fall through their fingers. Not only from my church but also through my contact with the Church worldwide, I have seen that this couple has not been alone in their struggle.

There are Christians everywhere doing without needed provision. Out of ignorance, they are setting a place at their table for the devourer. Jesus, as the Head of the Church, should be embraced as the Head of your table. If we serve Him first, there will be more than enough to go around.

When we disobey and rob God of His place, we bind His hands. He cannot defend us against the destroyer or devourer when we have withheld the first things. Could it be that this is the same spirit that was released in Egypt? Remember what happened with the plagues. The Bible says that God gave the Israelites a way to differentiate themselves from the Egyptians. God allowed the destroyer the right to enter the home of anyone who did not comply with His command.

Because the destroyer respects nothing but the blood of the Lamb, he was looking for one thing alone. And so God said, "If blood is on your door post, when the destroyer comes, he will pass over your house and your firstborn and all that you have will live."

Can you imagine how much money is wasted in the lives of believers as a result of the curses at work in our lives? But when we put Him first, He reverses the curse of the devourer and rebukes him for our sake, because He is Lord.

"...And I will rebuke the devourer for your sakes."

Malachi 3:11 NKJV

You can give offerings but that won't be enough if the devourer is not rebuked. When the children of Israel purged themselves of the "Achan factor", the blessing returned immediately. This might be a suggestion for some of us. If blessing wasn't in my life, I sure wouldn't try accusing God before I looked at my own heart.

God has put laws in place that are in effect whether we acknowledge them or not. If we violate these laws, the result will be a lack of blessing for which we often blame God. It's not God's fault. It may be Him allowing it, but it's not His fault.

He will simply say, "Shut off the blessing down there for awhile, because they've got to learn something. I love them and I have been merciful to them. My grace has covered them, the blood of Jesus applies to them, but I cannot let them by with that violation. If I do, it will be their destruction."

CHAPTER SUMMARY

- ISRAEL SLEW LAMBS ON THEIR THRESHOLDS ON THE EVE OF THEIR REDEMPTION FROM EGYPT, BUT JESUS WAS SACRIFICED ON THE THRESHOLD OF A NEW ERA.

- GOD NEVER INTENDED TO DO AWAY WITH THE LAW ITSELF. HIS INTENT WAS TO CHANGE OUR NATURES SO THAT THE SPIRIT OF THE LAW WAS WRITTEN IN OUR HEARTS AND MINDS.

- SIN NO LONGER REQUIRES DEATH FOR REDEMPTION. JESUS DIED ONCE FOR EVERYONE, AND IF THE DESTROYER SEES JESUS' BLOOD APPLIED TO YOUR LIFE, HE MUST PASS OVER YOU!

- ANYTIME THERE IS A REDEMPTIVE WORK IN PROGRESS, THERE WILL BE A NUMBER TEN INVOLVED.

- GOD HAD TO MAKE A WAY FOR THE GIVING OF FIRST THINGS IN A CASH ECONOMY.

- THE WORD *TITHE* MEANS 'TENTH'.

- WHY MUST IT BE FIRST? BECAUSE WHEN IT'S GIVEN FIRST IT BREAKS THE CURSE OF DESTRUCTION OFF OF THE REMAINING 90%, RELEASING IT TO BE USED FOR ITS BEST PURPOSE!

- TITHE IS GIVEN FIRST IN FAITH TO GUARANTEE GOD

THAT HE DESERVES FIRST PLACE BECAUSE OF WHO HE IS, NOT WHAT HE PROVIDES. IT MAY BE TEN PERCENT BUT IF IT IS NOT THE FIRST FRUITS IT DOESN'T COUNT AS TITHE, IT IS JUST AN OFFERING.

- ABEL BROUGHT AN OFFERING OF THE FIRSTBORN, BUT CAIN BROUGHT ONLY AN OFFERING OF SOME!

- ABEL PUT GOD FIRST, CAIN DID NOT.

- THE ORDER OF THAT WHICH IS GIVEN TO HIM CLEARLY DEFINES HIS PLACE IN YOUR LIFE.

- WHEN THE FIRST IS GIVEN, IT BUYS BACK (OR REDEEMS) ALL THAT REMAINS FROM THE CURSE OF DESTRUCTION.

- IT IS NOT AN ISSUE OF HEAVEN OR HELL. IT IS AN ISSUE OF SUCCESS OR FAILURE.

- IT IS IN KEEPING WHAT BELONGS TO GOD AND DENYING THE PROVISION AND PROTECTION OF LORDSHIP THAT IS THE CURSE.

- WHEN WE PUT HIM FIRST, HE REVERSES THE CURSE OF THE DEVOURER AND REBUKES HIM FOR OUR SAKE, BECAUSE HE IS LORD.

8

The Proof Is In The Paycheck

"Bring all the tithes — the whole tenth of
your income — into the storehouse, that
there may be food in My house, and prove
me now by it, says the Lord of hosts,
if I will not open the windows of heaven
for you and pour you our a blessing
that there shall not be room enough
to receive it."

MALACHI 3:10 AMPLIFIED

Chapter Eight

In the story of Cain and Abel we talked about God's response to the way we give. This time let's illustrate the "behind-the-scenes" response in heaven. Let me take a poetic license for a moment with regard to how prayer works. Take, for example, a prayer offered by the head of a family that may be facing family trouble or financial lack.

When the prayer is offered, it comes before God's throne of ultimate authority in Heaven sounding something like this, "Lord, my children are in trouble" or, "God, my job is at stake – and I can't afford to be laid off . . ."

The angels, who the Bible says are 'ministering spirits sent to the heirs of salvation', stand by waiting for their orders. And the Lord says, "Angels go get the record. I'm hearing from one of my children!" As the angel returns to the throne of God, he says, "'The first fruits, Father, have not been given. The spirit of Achan is present and they didn't give the first portion to You. They earn good income

Lord, and they are praying about losing their job, but they have been spending their tithe on their own pursuits. They seem to intend to give their tithe, but every week they run out of money before they get to You. Lord, it seems You are just too far back in the line."

In response, God says, "I am sorry for them, because the enemy has placed a curse on them, so that there will be failure, ignorance and barrenness instead of success, wisdom and abundance. My hands are tied because they have stolen the first fruits. I am not Lord in their life."

But you say, "Wait a minute! He is God, He is Sovereign and He can do anything He wants." No, no, God cannot do anything He wants. God has established laws and perimeters that He operates within, and He will not violate those laws. God chooses to live by laws that He has pre-established, and it is to our advantage to know those laws. The Law of First Things is the way God establishes His Lordship in the lives of His people from generation to generation.

THE PRACTICAL MEASURE

The choices we make concerning our time and the dispensing of our finances are two of the primary ways that we show God His place in our lives. God allots each of us so much time. Everybody has 24 hours in a day and seven days in a week.

People everywhere say, "Lord, Lord, You are Lord." Yet, in the dispensing of their time, they are stingy with God. How can a true believer complain about the length of a church service? If the service goes 30 seconds over the aloted time frame, people say, "This is the twenty-first century, and we have stuff to do, we have places to go and people to see." How can you feel that two hours in a church service is a long time, when by the same standard, it's not a long time to sit in a movie theater? How many Christians sit in front of the television for hours without blinking? It is very easy to sit down and waste two hours watching something on television that has little or no moral redeeming value.

If we were as hungry for the things of God as we ought to be, and if we really wanted to raise great kids, if we really wanted to change the world, if we really believed we are the righteousness of God in Christ, then not only would we not care about the length of the service, we might stay in church all afternoon seeking the face of God.

SUCCESS BEGINS ON SUNDAY

The early church understood the concept of giving the first portion of their time. The reason we have church on Sunday is not because Sunday is the Sabbath. In fact, Sunday is not the Sabbath. Saturday is, and has always been the Sabbath day. There is no commandment that changed the Sabbath to Sunday.

The reason we have church on Sunday is because the early church began gathering on the weekly anniversary of Jesus' resurrection to celebrate and worship. They decided they would rather devote the first fruits of their time to the Lord than to spend it on themselves. You see, in those days, Sunday was the first day of the work week. So while the unbelievers were out there trying to get ahead, the believers were giving the first day of the week to the Lord. They understood the importance of devoting the first fruits of their time to God as a redemptive offering for the rest of the week.

For some people, their week begins on Monday. They can't wait to get that first business deal started. For others, their week starts on Friday. They can't wait to finish their work week and start the weekend. They live to party! But for a Christian, our week starts on Sunday! The first day of the week we offer to worship.

As you can see, how we use our time clearly indicates what is truly first in our lives. We cannot control time. I don't care how many day-planners you have or clocks or watches. Time marches forward never to return. Yet, we have a glorious promise through the Law of First Things. Our time can be redeemed, and our success truly does begin on Sunday.

REALITY CHECK

Money is a means to an end. Dollars and cents just happen to be the commodity in our society that equals time spent. Time spent working on your job is in turn translated into money or a paycheck.

When you give the first portion of that money to God, that is the closest you will ever come to human sacrifice.

When you tithe you are literally giving yourself. If giving is an indication of Lordship then how do you think we are doing as the Body of Christ? Let's look at some statistics.

The most recent survey taken shows that only 18% of Christians in America tithe in any form, and that includes those who "think" they are tithing. Let me give you some statistics that I think you will find both shocking and disappointing. I recently received the latest figures available on worldwide giving, from the compilers of the new "World Christian Encyclopedia" (Oxford University Press AD 2000).

In 1998, global Christian income was $15.2 trillion U.S. dollars. Globally, Christians gave $270 billion U.S. dollars to churches and para-church organizations. That amounts to 1.8% of total income. Believe it or not, the United States did less than that! Because we are the most prosperous nation in the world, I really believed we "carried" the rest of the global church by supporting at a much higher rate. I was surprised.

The total U.S. income of Christians in 1998 was $5.2 trillion U.S. dollars. In the United States, Christians gave $92 billion U.S. dollars to their churches and all Christian para-church organizations. That equals 1.78% of our collective income. That means that even though God has blessed us to live in the most prosperous nation in the history of mankind, we collectively give less, by percentage, than the rest of the world.

By revealing these statistics, I am not trying to bring condemnation upon Christians. I just want to prompt a reality check. I want to remind you of the challenge in Malachi 3:10, when the Lord said to prove Him with the tithe, not pay Him with it. He is daring you to apply the Law of First Things and see what happens. When you do this— be prepared. He warns that you will not have room to contain the blessing that follows.

BUILDING BIGGER BARNS

I find it interesting that one of the biggest investment opportunities in America is to invest in temporary storage facilities. If you'll notice, they are springing up everywhere. We have so much "stuff" that we need to rent warehouses to store it for us. Jesus said our lives do not consist in the abundance of "stuff" we have. Jesus described a rich man in Luke 12, that found himself in the same dilemma which many of us today are in. He possessed so much stuff that his barns wouldn't hold it all.

His decision was to tear down his barns and build bigger barns. It is too bad that this man did not have a cause or a purpose to his life higher than that—the storage of stuff. Jesus called him a fool. Jesus asked the rich man the question we should ask ourselves, "The night your soul is required of you, who will this stuff belong to?"

I long to see the day when the Body of Christ will resign from the quest for excess and begin to pass our extra provision on to the ones who need it. I want you to remember this: if there is no Lord in your life, there is no redemption in your life. And if there is no redemption at work in your life and you don't know what to do with your life, then your life is meaningless.

IT'S NOT ABOUT MONEY

This is not about money at all. If you think it is, then you have missed the whole point of this message. It is no more about money now than it was about sheep in the Old Testament. It is about Lordship. If He is Lord, you are redeemed. If He is not Lord, you are under the curse of the devourer. Does God not love you? Certainly He loves you; that is the reason Jesus died for you. You see, it is not a matter of His love for us   it's a matter of His Lordship in our lives.

Remember the prayer offered to God, and His response to the one who did not give the first portion? Now, after hearing and applying the message, let's change the story around a little. . . There is prayer offered by the same head of this family and God says, "Angel, go check the records." The angel comes back, grinning from ear to ear, and says, "Lord, there have been some tough times and they didn't always know how they were going to do it, but You are first in their life because they always gave the First portion!"

I can just see the Father rejoice and say, "Because I am first, I have the opportunity to set in motion the redemptive factor and divine provision. Since the First Fruits was given, there will be success, not failure; peace of mind, not depression; fruitfulness, not barrenness; intelligence, not ignorance; healthy babies, not miscarriage; wealth, not poverty; a strong marriage, not divorce; health, not sickness; life and not death!" This is the redemptive release!

DIVINE PROVISION

I think everyone should experience those times when God comes through for you. I had just such an experience as a young pastor, just after starting our church. After renting an old bank building for our services, we managed to buy a much-needed air conditioner. A precious man from the area volunteered to install it on the following Saturday and he called me the evening before and told me what supplies to bring.

I had everything he mentioned – except a roll of copper tubing. And not only did I not have the copper tubing, I had no money to buy it with. At first, I anticipated being embarrassed, but then I recalled the miraculous ways God had already provided since I had chosen to put Him first in my life and ministry. Deciding to trust God and deal with the matter in the morning, I fell into a peaceful sleep.

Driving to the church early the next morning, it was so foggy I could hardly see. Still trying to wake up, I stopped at a red light. While waiting for the light, I looked out the side window and there lying beside my car in the middle of the street was a roll of copper tubing. I couldn't believe it! I got out, picked up the copper tubing and put it in the back of my car.

When I arrived at the church, we began to install the air conditioning unit. When it came time to connect the two parts the installer asked me if I had brought the copper tubing. I ran to the car and brought it to him. He ran it from the root unit down to the inside unit and it fit almost perfectly. After he cut off about four inches of extra tubing, he said, "You really figured this close." I laughed and said, "You don't know how close!" I shared the story of God's divine provision with him and we rejoiced together.

In monetary value, that copper tubing was only worth about 50 dollars but it was worth a million dollars to me! God will provide when you put Him first!

CHAPTER SUMMARY

- GOD HAS ESTABLISHED LAWS AND PERIMETERS THAT HE OPERATES WITHIN, AND HE WILL NOT VIOLATE THOSE LAWS.

- THE CHOICES WE MAKE CONCERNING OUR TIME AND THE DISPENSING OF OUR FINANCES ARE TWO OF THE PRIMARY WAYS THAT WE SHOW GOD HIS PLACE IN OUR LIVES.

- FOR A CHRISTIAN, OUR WEEK STARTS ON SUNDAY! THE FIRST DAY OF THE WEEK WE OFFER TO WORSHIP.

- OUR TIME CAN BE REDEEMED AND OUR SUCCESS TRULY DOES BEGIN ON SUNDAY.

- WHEN YOU GIVE THE FIRST PORTION TO GOD, THAT IS THE CLOSEST YOU WILL EVER COME TO HUMAN SACRIFICE.

- ONLY 18% OF CHRISTIANS IN AMERICA TITHE IN ANY FORM, AND THAT INCLUDES THOSE WHO "THINK" THEY ARE TITHING.

- EVEN THOUGH GOD HAS BLESSED US TO LIVE IN THE MOST PROSPEROUS NATION IN THE HISTORY OF MANKIND, WE COLLECTIVELY GIVE LESS, BY PERCENTAGE, THAN THE REST OF THE WORLD.

- THE LORD SAID TO *PROVE HIM* WITH THE TITHE, NOT *PAY HIM* WITH IT.

- I LONG TO SEE THE DAY WHEN THE BODY OF CHRIST WILL RESIGN FROM THE QUEST FOR EXCESS AND BEGIN TO PASS OUR EXTRA PROVISION ON TO THE ONES WHO NEED IT.

- IF THERE IS NO REDEMPTION AT WORK IN YOUR LIFE AND YOU DON'T KNOW WHAT TO DO WITH YOUR LIFE, THEN YOUR LIFE IS MEANINGLESS.

- THIS IS NOT ABOUT MONEY AT ALL.

- IT IS ABOUT LORDSHIP.

- IT IS NOT A MATTER OF HIS LOVE FOR US – IT'S A MATTER OF HIS LORDSHIP IN OUR LIVES.

9

How Great The Commission

"Go ye therefore and make disciples of all the nations, baptizing them in the name of the Father and of the Son and of the Holy Spirit, teaching them to observe all things that I have commanded you..."

MATTHEW 28:19 NKJV

Chapter Nine

For 4,000 years, God dealt almost exclusively with the Jewish people as a nation. His covenant with them was designed for several reasons. One, to exemplify the kind of care and concern God has for those He commits Himself to. Secondly, He wanted to show that every covenant or agreement between two parties always carries two-way responsibility. The promises of God to Israel were always conditional. "If you will... then I will," was usually the way every promise was worded.

We have to remember as New Testament Christians that God did not offer covenant relationship to all the people on the earth at that time. His covenant was exclusively with Israel. In fact, the term 'Gentile' literally means 'one who has no covenant with God.'

Israel was God's example nation among all the nations. God's amazing interventions on behalf of His people, from the dividing of the Red Sea, to the sun standing still for an entire day at Joshua's request, were examples of His faithfulness to those He loves.

Then, 2,000 years ago, Jesus came to the earth to open a new chapter in God's dealings with Man on the earth. After reaching the age of 30, Jesus began His public ministry. That ministry was designed for one purpose – to convince not just the Israelites but the entire world of God's love. Through Christ, God was inviting the Gentiles, those who had no covenant, to come into covenant relationship with Him.

Jesus' sacrifice was the price paid for the sins of mankind. That is why John the Baptist said of Jesus, "Behold the Lamb of God that takes away the sins of the world!" Your sin and mine was taken away by Jesus.

If you are not in relationship with God, this is a good place to stop and receive the precious gift of salvation! Just thank God for offering you the gift of salvation, free. Confess Him as your Lord, Savior, and Master. Admit that you are a sinner – He already paid for your sins. He will accept you instantly into His family.

As Jesus prepared to birth the New Testament church before His ascension to the Father, He commanded His disciples to *"go ye into all the world and preach the gospel to all people"* (Matt 28:19). We call this "The Great Commission."

As much as God cared for the Nation of Israel in the Old Testament, they had no "Great Commission." We do! The Great Commission was

God's invitation for all, both Jews and Gentiles. As exciting as this is, this is a huge responsibility! Can you imagine how much money, how many millions of lives, how much sacrifice, how much pain and weariness, how many tragedies have been invested in the mission to fulfill that commandment?

If God required the tithe of Old Testament Israel, when they had no 'Great Commission' to reach the world, how much more should we in the New Testament Church be committed to a plan of giving to fund the most massive outreach ever attempted?

The Apostle Paul had the right plan. I Corinthians 16:2 says, *"On the first day of each week, let each one of you put aside something and save it up as he has prospered in proportion to what he is given-so that no collection will need to be taken after I come."* AMPLIFIED

Let us look at a list of the specifics of Paul's instruction.

FIRST DAY OF EACH WEEK—FIRST FRUITS of your time

EACH ONE OF YOU—TOTAL PARTICIPATION

LAY ASIDE AN OFFERING—PREPARED GIVING

AS GOD HAS PROSPERED YOU—PROPORTIONATE OR PERCENTAGE GIVING

NO SPECIAL COLLECTION WILL BE NEEDED

This is the ingenious plan of God. If every

Christian would simply give God the first fruits (the first 10% of all they earn) there would be no need for "special collections". Fundraising projects would be eliminated.

My second born grandson is now three years old. As many grandparents know, things they say can be either frightening or enlightening. On a Sunday morning a while back, his mother tucked his offering in his pocket and sent him to Sunday school with a reminder to give it. Later on, when his mother picked him up from class she asked him, "Stacen, did you give your offering to Jesus?" and he worriedly replied, "No Mommy, I gave it to the bucket!"

After we all had a good laugh, I thought about his answer. I think because most people put their offering into a bucket or a plate, they fail to see who their money is really given to. Jesus and his Church should be the heartbeat of our existence. If we all gave the way God designed, we would have enough resource to reach the whole world and still be able to meet needs at home! Accept the personal challenge.

JUST IMAGINE

One of the most important things we can do is dream. It is often not easy to do. Today is a good example. I came up to our ranch retreat to write this chapter. God has blessed our church with a beautiful, 120 acre get-away, about an hour from Dallas. As you probably know, however, there is a lot to do in maintaining a ranch property. I got up early this morning and got started. I trimmed some trees, cleared some brush, hauled some trash, watered the lawn and killed a snake—all before breakfast!

Kathy was getting ready to return home ahead of me. When I told her I was going to write this chapter before I headed home, she said, "You won't get to it; you have too many distractions."

She didn't intend to hurt my feelings, but she did. After all, just last night we were sitting out under the stars, after enjoying a beautiful sunset, talking about how much we loved each other. I told Kathy then, and I still mean it, how much I appreciate her sharing her life with me. She is truly the most enjoyable companion in the world to me. She is so easy to be with. But she challenged me when she told me I wasn't going to get this chapter written that day.

There is a point to this story. The point is this – here I was, in the middle of a peaceful environment, my capable church staff covering for me at home, and I was working like crazy on everything but the book. That is the reason I came up here! It is so difficult to find time to dream. Do you find it difficult? It seems that one of the curses of this modern era is busy-ness.

I titled this section "Just Imagine" because it is important for us to take a little "dream time" to capture the reality of the opportunity before us. In the time of Jesus' earthly ministry, there is only one place that Jesus specifically requested prayer. In Matt 9:37, He said, *"The harvest truly is plentiful, but the laborers are few. Therefore, pray the Lord of the Harvest to send out laborers into His harvest."* {NKJV}

I am not sure if He were with us today, that this would still be His prayer request. After all, we have been praying that prayer now for centuries. I believe that prayer has largely been answered. Today there seems to be churches full of willing laborers all over the world. I believe if Jesus were with us today He would say, "The laborers are many, but they have no support. Pray that the Lord of the harvest will send a spirit of obedience and generosity on the church to support the work of the harvest."

The statistics I shared with you earlier reveal several things. One, they reveal that we are not serious about taking the gospel to the whole world. Do we really believe that 1.8% of our income is an earnest investment in the furtherance of the Kingdom?

Secondly, we can see that if we are accomplishing what is being done with only 1.8% of our income, what could we accomplish if we truly gave the "first fruits" of all our increase? If you do the math on these statistics you will discover a six factor. That means that if we just tithed properly, every ministry, church, pastor, missionary, Christian media ministry would have six times more income to accomplish their mission than they currently have.

Let me give you an example. Our giving income last year at Covenant Church was over $10 million dollars. If you apply a six factor, we would have had $60 million to work with to reach our community instead of $10 million.

I simply want to ask: "What is possible when God is FIRST? Can you imagine?" Dream for a moment. Just imagine, if every believer simply tithed, we would possess so much provision, we could literally change the way "ministry" is viewed. What would the world be like if every church, prison ministry, youth home, crisis pregnancy center, TV ministry and missions organization had six times more finances to work with? It is possible. All it takes is the decision of every believer to honor God with the first fruits of their increase. I not only believe it is possible, I believe God has called me to be a voice - not of condemnation, but of hope, faith and possibility. We can do it! I am providing a necessary foundational understanding to begin our imaginary journey. Are you ready? Let's go.

Imagine - every local church having its own school through university level with free education to every member.

Imagine - every local church could staff its own medical clinic with care made available free of charge to all its members.

Imagine - every church having a youth center with state of the art equipment from movie theatres to sports facilities—ministering to the young people of our communities free!

Imagine - every church being able to send missionaries and fully funding them so they don't have to spend most of their time raising financial support.

Imagine - having enough money to buy out your local abortion clinic and turn it into a birthing center where every baby born is adopted and loved by Christian parents.

Imagine - every church being able to provide support for single parents that would allow them to stay home and raise their children!

It is possible!

If we must return to reality for a moment, I believe we can discover the major reasons why the percent of "first fruits" tithing is so low. First of all, there is a lack of revelational teaching. If the ministry does not possess a "word", the people will not be released to walk in it. The scripture says, *"You will know the truth and the truth (you know) will set you free."* John 8:32 AMPLIFIED

Secondly, there is fear on the part of the ministry to boldly challenge the people to give. Many times others in ministry have shared with me that receiving the offering is the most difficult part of the service for them to do. It is because of the fear of criticism. That fear is not without reason.

Many precious, dedicated men of God have been personally attacked, as though the offering is all for them, by cruel, selfish people who didn't want their stinginess challenged. The natural reaction is to fold your tent and try to accomplish your ministry mandate without ever mentioning money again. It cannot be done. Jesus spoke more about money than heaven or hell!

Finally, the "deceitfulness of riches" is the reason we, as the church, don't do more giving than we do. What is the "deceitfulness of riches" as referred to in Matt. 13:22? Riches deceive by convincing you of their power to supply happiness, security and fulfillment. They simply cannot. But in our relentless search for significance, we often weary ourselves by seeking something that, in the end, cannot deliver.

On the other hand, if we pursue wealth with the idea that we are a pipeline of blessing through which resources can flow to bless the Kingdom, then everyone wins! It has been said that you don't have a life worth living if you haven't found a cause worth dying for. I have found that cause. My small place in the ever increasing Kingdom of God is a cause worth dying for...but guess what? I have not been asked to die, but to live for the cause. Because Jesus already died, we are called to live for His glory.

Take a moment to examine your own life. Where do you fit into the statistical picture I shared earlier? Did you do more or less than the worldwide average of 1.8% giving?

I guess a better question is, did you take a moment to dream? If you did, I hope you are captured by the vision of the kind of world it would be if the Kingdom of God had 6 times more provision at our disposal. Don't ever stop dreaming that dream! When we wake up soon in the presence of the Lord, it will be worth more than you can ever dream to hear Him say, "Well done, good and faithful servant, enter into the joy of the Lord."

CHAPTER SUMMARY

- EVERY COVENANT OR AGREEMENT BETWEEN TWO PARTIES ALWAYS CARRIES TWO-WAY RESPONSIBILITY.

- AS MUCH AS GOD CARED FOR THE NATION OF ISRAEL IN THE OLD TESTAMENT, THEY HAD NO "GREAT COMMISSION", WE DO!

- IF EVERY CHRISTIAN WOULD SIMPLY GIVE GOD THE FIRST FRUITS (THE FIRST 10% OF ALL THEY EARN) THERE WOULD BE NO NEED FOR "SPECIAL COLLECTIONS".

- IF WE ALL GAVE THE WAY GOD DESIGNED, WE WOULD HAVE ENOUGH RESOURCE TO REACH THE WHOLE WORLD AND STILL BE ABLE TO MEET NEEDS AT HOME!

- IT IS IMPORTANT FOR US TO TAKE A LITTLE "DREAM TIME" TO CAPTURE THE REALITY OF THE OPPORTUNITY BEFORE US.

- IF WE JUST TITHED PROPERLY, EVERY MINISTRY, CHURCH, PASTOR, MISSIONARY, CHRISTIAN MEDIA MINISTRY WOULD HAVE SIX TIMES MORE INCOME TO ACCOMPLISH THEIR MISSION

- THE "DECEITFULNESS OF RICHES" IS THE REASON WE, AS THE CHURCH, DON'T DO MORE GIVING THAN WE DO.

- YOU DON'T HAVE A LIFE WORTH LIVING IF YOU HAVEN'T FOUND A CAUSE WORTH DYING FOR.

10
Redemptive Work In Progress

"O Israel, put your hope in the Lord, for with the Lord is unfailing love and with him is full redemption."

PSALMS 130:7 NIV

Chapter Ten

Right away, one of two things is going to happen. Either your flesh, with logic and reasoning, is going to figure out an excuse to twist this message around to make it into something confusing or you will feel an urgency to claim all God has for you.

I hope this message reverberates in your spirit, and I hope it affects you the next time you write a check or pay your tithe. I hope that you can decide today that it is just time and money, but He is God and He is worth first place!

You will make a decision that will affect the inhabitants of this earth for all eternity. Your decision will cause people that have yet to be reached, to have the opportunity to make Him Lord.

We only have so much time in this world to make a difference. Are we intent on making a difference, or are we just along for the ride? Are we people that want to be kings and priests unto God, or are we just patty-caking for Jesus?

Are we just looking for fire insurance or are we serious about changing a hurting world?

If we reached the level of commitment to say, "If God didn't play games with The Law of First Things, then I'm not going to play games with it either."

Reading this book is only the beginning of the journey of blessing that is there for those who honor God. Your application of the Law of First Things will determine the ending of this book. Success or failure is yet to be written— by you. The redemptive work of this message will not be complete until you receive it and His place in your life is clearly defined as FIRST.

MY GOALS FOR GIVING

- I RECOGNIZE GOD AS THE RIGHTFUL OWNER OF ALL THAT I POSSESS.

- GOD KNOWS WHAT I NEED BEFORE I EVER ASK.

- I WILL WORK WITH DILIGENCE AND WISDOM TO EARN INCOME.

- I WILL OFFER TO HIM THE FIRST FRUITS (10%) OF ALL THAT HE BLESSES ME WITH.

- I WILL GIVE OFFERINGS FROM THE PORTION THAT REMAINS.

- I WILL GRATEFULLY ACCEPT THE HARVEST THAT WILL BE RETURNED TO ME.

- I WILL ENCOURAGE THOSE WHO MAY DOUBT THAT CONSISTENT GIVING WILL REAP A REWARD.

TOP 10 QUESTIONS ON TITHING

1. *Do I tithe on the gross amount of my income or the net?*

Tithe on the gross. The difference between the gross and the net includes benefits to you like health insurance, government supplied roads, police and fire, etc.

2. *Isn't the concept of tithing an Old Testament law that was not taught in the New Testament scriptures?*

The principle of tithing is actually older than the old covenant because Abraham paid tithes to Mechizedek in Gen. 14. Jesus endorsed the paying of the tithe in Matt. 23:23. Also, Paul, the apostle, in I Cor. 16:2 said, "On the first day of each week let each one of you bring an offering as God hath prospered you." This is speaking of percentage or proportionate giving.

3. *What if my spouse is not saved and does not allow me to tithe?*

You are not held accountable for what you do not possess. I would suggest, however, two options. First, don't just assume your spouse won't allow it. Choose a time to appeal to him/her and ask if you can give a regular portion of income. Secondly, if you do not have money to give, give time to the ministry of your choice and God will honor it.

4. *I own a business. How do I tithe from my business?*

Tithing is computed based on increase or profit. There are several ways to compute profits and certain times when that can be done. Work out the details with your accountant. I believe God is calling large numbers of Christians to start businesses for the purpose of furthering His kingdom.

5. *Where should my tithe be paid - all to my church or part of it to a missions cause or media ministry?*

The scripture says in Mal. 3, "Bring all the tithes into the storehouse that there may be meat in My house." This is normally translated to mean the local church. Many people however, are not connected to a local church. In that case try to make sure there is an accountable leader responsible to administer finances in a godly manner.

6. Do all the tithes belong to the pastor or minister?

The scripture says in Num. 18:24 that the tithes are for the Levites which were the ministry tribe. That does not mean, however, that all of the tithe is to be used by the pastor. Only one Levite functioned as the high priest and hundreds of others did the "work of the ministry." Their work was also supported out of the tithe. The minister or pastor in a New Testament church should be supported by and administrate the tithes to the effectiveness of all the work of the ministry. Tithe should not be paid to any organization that is not directed by God-called ministry.

7. Is the tithe limited to just ten percent?

No, even though this is where it begins you can add to the percentage of your income that you tithe, as you wish. Although the word, tithe, by definition means 10%, it is said that J.C. Penney, the founder of the store chain, was tithing 90% of his income and retired a wealthy man. Begin by praying that God will double and triple the amount you give as tithe. So that 10% of your income will be twice or three times as much money.

8. *What if I am in a situation where there is financial abuse?*

God will never hold you accountable for the performance of those stewards He placed over you. God will judge His servants. You pray for them and remain faithful.

9. *Should ministers pay tithe?*

Yes, for two reasons. First, because as a leader we must be examples. Secondly, the scriptures say in Num. 18:26, *"When you Levites take tithes from the Israelites which I have given you from them for an inheritance, then you shall present an offering from it to the Lord, even a tenth of the tithe".*

10. What if I have not been tithing properly?

This is the beauty of New Testament grace. In the Old Testament you would be punished. Because of the forgiveness we have through Jesus' blood, you simply repent and purpose in your heart to begin now being faithful in giving the tithe from this day forward.

AUDIO TEACHINGS FROM MIKE HAYES!

God's Answer for Racial Reconciliation

How do we as people of the church aide in racial reconciliation?

Amazing Grace

A study on knowing the plan of God. Why wrath and grace? This series also teaches about whether you would rather be pardoned or justified.

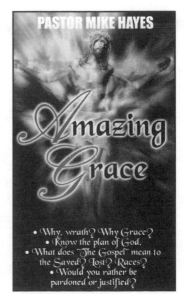

Blessings and Curses

Understanding and removing curses from our lives and filling the void with an anointing the Bible calls "Blessing".

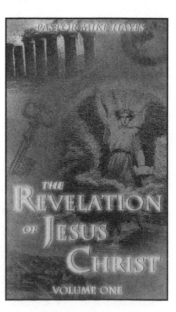

Revelation Series Volumes 1,2,and 3

Dynamic teaching on the book of Revelation, Chapters 1-10.

This is a study of us personally and the plan of God for our lives. Each volume contains 6 audio cassettes.

ABOUT THE AUTHOR:

With little more than a vision a young wife, two-year old daughter and a fish tank, Mike Hayes ventured to the Dallas--Fort Worth metroplex. His mission--to reach the lost, didn't seem impossible because he had been promised he would be sent "a team" to help in making the vision reality. God was faithful and now in the North Dallas suburb of Carrollton stands a beautiful church called "Covenant" which houses a "team" approaching ten thousand.

His purpose in life is evident by the overwhelming harvest attributed to the expository word that comes from more than thirty years of ministry experience. Mike Hayes is a messenger with an easily understood, timely word addressing the most difficult of issues in the Body of Christ today.

He makes his home in north Dallas, with his wife Kathy. They have a daughter, Amie, and a son, Stephen, Stacey, their son-in-law and four grandchildren, Grayson, Stacen, Tate and Molly-Kate, and an extended family of multiple thousands.

For additional copies of this book, write:

ALBURY PUBLISHING
P.O. Box 470406
Tulsa, OK 74147-0406

To contact the author, write:

Mike Hayes Ministries
2644 East Trinity Mills Road
Carrollton, TX 75006

or
visit his website:

www.covenantchurch.org